UNIQUE WOMAN

INSIGHT AND WISDOM TO MAXIMIZE YOUR LIFE

MAJORING IN MEN®

The Curriculum for Men

by
Edwin Louis Cole and
Nancy Corbett Cole

RESOLUTE BOOKS

Southlake, Texas

UNIQUE WOMAN WORKBOOK:
Insight and Wisdom to Maximize Your Life

Christian Men's Network
P.O. Box 93478
Southlake, TX 76092
www.ChristianMensNetwork.com

Facebook.com/EdwinLouisCole

ISBN: 978-1-93862-920-4
Printed in the United States of America
© 2014 Edwin and Nancy Cole Legacy LLC

Published by:
Resolute Books™
1030 Hunt Valley Circle
New Kensington, PA 15068

Majoring in Men® and Resolute Books™ is a registered trademark of Edwin and Nancy Cole Legacy LLC.

2 3 4 5 6 7 8 9 10 11 / 20 19 18 17

TABLE OF CONTENTS

Lesson 1
The Uniqueness of the Woman

Lesson 1
The Uniqueness of the Woman

A. Both men and women have a God-given _____. *(fill in the blank)* *(page 15)*

    annoying habit   uniqueness   problem to overcome

1. Men and women are a complement to each other. *(page 15)*

    ___ True   ___ False

2. Statistically, how many women are probably abused? *(page 16)*

    _____

3. Name some results in women's lives from abuse, hurt or sexual molestation. *(pages 16-17)*

    _____

    _____

    _____

4. How do small gestures like birthday and anniversary cards make a woman feel? *(page 17)*

    _____

For Further Study

See dictionary definitions for *unique* – "*One and only, having no like or equal, unparalleled, highly unusual, extraordinary, rare.*" Compare to Psalm 139:13-18.

Satan's pattern – Damaging, perverting, robbing and limiting women – Genesis 3; "*The thief cometh not, but for to steal, and to kill, and to destroy*" John 10:10; "*Be sober, be vigilant; because your adversary the devil, as a roaring lion, walketh about, seeking whom he may devour*" 1 Peter 5:8.

B. Every man or woman has a _____,_____ hunger. *(fill in the blank) (page 17)*

recognition   deprivation   self-involvement

1. Circle the correct response for a man when his wife asks, *"Do you love me?"* *(page 18)*

    a. *"Yeah"*   b. *"I did when we married; if it changes, I'll tell you."*

    c. *"Is the sky blue; is water wet; are mountains high? That's how much I love you!"*

2. What satisfies a woman's sense of uniqueness? *(circle all that apply) (page 18)*

    a. sex   b. worth   c. gifts   d. love

3. Why do some ministers' wives resent the church or ministry? *(pages 18-19)*

    _____

    What is the antidote to cure this?

    _____

4. A life without value is _____. *(page 19)*

For Further Study

People need to feel loved and valued. Reward workers – 1 Corinthians 9:7-10; 1 Timothy 5:18.
Ministers' wives who work alongside their husbands deserve compensation and a sense of value (Reap where you sow spiritually) – Romans 15:27, 28 TLB; 1 Corinthians 9:11, 13-14.
The rewards of hard work – Proverbs 13:11, 12; *"For the workman deserves his support (his living, his food)"* Matthew 10:10 AMP.

C. Write the letter of the word that best completes the sentences. *(pages 19-20)*

____ 1. Men and women derive satisfaction from   a. completion

____ 2. Adam was given stewardship over the   b. imparting revelation and eternal life

____ 3. A man's uniqueness is basically fulfilled in his   c. reproductive process on earth

____ 4. Jesus was replenished in energy by   d. different sources

____ 5. For love to exist, there must be an   e. object to love

____ 6. Women were created as the man's   f. job

D. Where did Adam's characteristics come from? *(page 20)* _____

1. Adam had the nature of God in him, including the tender and tough, the disciplinarian and nurturer. *(page 20)*

___ True ___ False

2. If God had created the woman from anything other than that which was already in Adam, she would have been inferior to the man. *(page 20)*

___ True ___ False

For Further Study

God reveals the equality in the creation of man and woman – Genesis 1:26-27; 2:23; Ephesians 5:28-29; *"In the Lord, however, woman is not independent of man, nor is man independent of woman"* 1 Corinthians 11:11 NIV. The rib is symbolic of characteristics God took to make the woman's nature – *"She shall be called Woman, because she was taken out of Man"* Genesis 2:23; *"For as the woman is from the man, even so is the man also by the woman; but all things of God"* 1 Corinthians 11:12.

3.   Whom did God call "Adam"? *(page 21)*

   _____

4.   How is a woman's uniqueness basically satisfied? *(page 21)*

   _____

E.   One problem in marriage is that men and women generally do not appreciate each other's

   _____ or _____. *(page 21)*

   1.   Women dream of the ideal and marry the _____ man. *(page 21)*

   2.   Memorize: "Disappointments are not based on what you find, but on what you expect to find."
       (page 21) When did you personally experience this?

   _____

   3.   After marriage, do most men continue courtship? *(page 21)*   ___ Yes ___ No

   4.   What is one of the great dangers in marriage? *(page 22)* _____

   _____

For Further Study

Women – Genesis 3:16; Ephesians 5:24; *"A virtuous and capable wife ... is worth more than precious rubies"*
Proverbs 31:10 NLT.
Worth in relation to a husband – Proverbs 31:11, 12
Demanding satisfaction from your spouse indicates a lack of love – 1 Corinthians 10:24, 33; 13:4-7.
Loving adds to; demanding takes from – Luke 6:38; Romans 12:6-8; 13:9-10.

5. Today's society puts heavy burdens on both men and women. What are they? *(page 22)*

   Men: _____

   Women: _____

   What is the result in women? *(page 22)*

   _____

6. There is a rest in the _____ that frees us from the burden of the _____.
   (page 22)

For Further Study

Family members can pressure us to conform to their images of us – Luke 10:38-42.
Set priorities – Romans 12:2; Ephesians 5:15-17.
Resting in the eternal frees us from the burden of the temporal – Matthew 6:25-34.
God desires our highest good – Psalm 37:1-4; Proverbs 23:18; Jeremiah 29:11.

Practical:

1. What are your thoughts regarding God having both the male and female qualities? Discuss with your spouse or a friend the completeness of God and how men and women equally express His image.

   _____

2. Write your opinion on whether women are inferior to men. In what way(s) are they weaker? Stronger?

   _____

   _____

   _____

3. When was the last time you took your spouse away alone? Plan NOW!

   _____

Repeat this prayer out loud:

Father, thank You for giving me a new revelation about men and women and the image of God we both express. Please change all my wrong thinking and attitudes toward women as I study to show myself approved to You. In Jesus' Name, Amen.

Principles I want to memorize:

Self Test *Lesson 1*

1. Men have a greater uniqueness about them than women do.

    ___ True ___ False

2. Give some reasons why some women never enjoy the true freedom of being uniquely a woman:

    _____

    _____

3. Define "recognition hunger."

    _____

4. A life without value is: *(circle one)*

    a. worthless   b. livable   c. happier

5. Name some of Adam's traits before Eve was created:

    _____

6. How is a woman's uniqueness basically satisfied?

    _____

7. What are disappointments normally based on?

    _____

8. How do men sometimes change in their attitude toward their wives, from courtship to marriage?

    _____

Keep this test for your records.

Lesson 2
A Woman of God

Lesson 2
A Woman of God

A. Fill in the blanks. Five sins prohibit: *(page 28)*

men from being _____.

marriages from being _____.

nations from achieving _____ or _____.

1. Women have to overcome the same five sins. *(page 28)* ___ True ___ False

2. Name the five sins that kept Israel out of Canaan. *(page 28)*

   a. _____   d. _____

   b. _____   e. _____

   c. _____

3. Read 1 Corinthians 10.

For Further Study
Becoming wise – *"Every prudent man acts out of knowledge, but a fool exposes his folly"* Proverbs 13:16 NIV; *"O ye simple, understand wisdom: and, ye fools, be ye of an understanding heart"* Proverbs 8:5.
Five basic sins – Exodus 32:1-10; 19-35; Numbers 14; 25:1-9; Romans 1:18-32; 1 Corinthians 6:9-10; Hebrews 3:7-19; Jude 7; Revelation 22:15
Warnings – Romans 6:12; 13:13-14; 1 Corinthians 6:18; Colossians 3:5; 1 Peter 2:11; 1 John 5:2

B.   Define "lust." *(page 29)*

_____

_____

1.   Name two types of lust. *(page 29)*

a. _____   b. _____

2.   Define "lasciviousness." *(page 29)*

_____

3.   Read aloud 1 John 2:16.

4.   Name the three basic temptations. *(page 30)*

a. _____

b. _____

c. _____

For Further Study

Lustful synonyms – Excessive, loose, lewd, offensive sexual desire; unrestrained gratification of senses and bodily appetites; wanton, careless, undisciplined, unmanageable, senseless, unjustifiable, unlearned, ignorant, unprincipled behavior; reckless or arrogant disregard for justice, decency and morality; 2 Peter 2:13, 14; 1 John 2:15, 16.

Godly lifestyle – *"Whoever heard me spoke well of me, and those who saw me commended me ... I put on righteousness as my clothing; justice was my robe and my turban ... I made a covenant with my eyes not to look lustfully at a girl"* Job 29:11, 14; 31:1 NIV.

Warnings – Proverbs 6:25-26; Matthew 5:28; Colossians 3:5

C.   What sins have been the problem of the Church since the 1980s? *(page 30)*

      _____

1.   Define "fornication." *(page 30)*

      _____

2.   What is the "great deception of our day"? *(page 31)*

      _____

      _____

3.   Write out 1 John 3:6.

      _____

      _____

      _____

For Further Study

Sex Sins – *"But fornication, and all uncleanness, or covetousness, let it not be once named among you, as becometh saints"* Ephesians 5:3; Psalm 101:2-8; Romans 6; 1 Corinthians 6:18-20; Galatians 5:16-24; *"It is God's will that you should be sanctified: that you should avoid sexual immorality; that each of you should learn to control his own body in a way that is holy and honorable, not in passionate lust like the heathen, who do not know God"* 1 Thessalonians 4:3-5 NIV; Ephesians 4:17-19; 5:15-17; 1 Timothy 3:15; Titus 2:12-14; 1 John 2:3-6; 5:18; 3 John 11.

4. Compare/contrast someone who commits sin and someone who practices sin. *(page 31)*

_____

_____

_____

D. Give an example of tempting Christ. *(page 31)*

_____

E. Circle all of the following that are forms of idolatry: *(pages 31-32)*

   a. way of life   b. possessions   c. pornography   d. home

F. Circle all of the following that are forms of murmuring: *(pages 32-33)*

   a. cattiness   c. criticizing   e. backbiting   g. gossiping

   b. faultfinding   d. nagging   f. complaining   h. "sharing" prayer needs

For Further Study

Idolatry and murmuring – *"For of this you can be sure: No immoral, impure or greedy person—such a man is an idolater—has any inheritance in the kingdom of Christ and of God"* Ephesians 5:5 NIV; 1 Corinthians 10:14; Hebrews 13:5; 1 John 5:21; Revelation 21:7-8; *"Death and life are in the power of the tongue"* Proverbs 18:21; Proverbs 11:9, 12, 13; 12:18; 15:4; 20:19; Ephesians 4:29; 2 Timothy 2:16; *"A wise man's heart guides his mouth"* Proverbs 16:23 NIV; *"Pleasant words are as an honeycomb, sweet to the soul, and health to the bones"* Proverbs 16:24; *"Words from a wise man's mouth are gracious, but a fool is consumed by his own lips"* Ecclesiastes 10:12 NIV; *"Let the words of my mouth, and the meditation of my heart, be acceptable in thy sight, O Lord, my strength, and my redeemer"* Psalm 19:14.

Don't be idle – 2 Thessalonians 3:6-15; *"Going about from house to house … gossips and busybodies, saying things they ought not to"* 1 Timothy 5:13 NIV.

In your own words, why are gossip and murmuring so destructive to a church? *(pages 32-33)*

_____

_____

G.   How does a woman best find her identity? *(pages 35-36)*

_____

1.   Read Matthew 10:39.

2.   Women cannot identify with Christ as men can because Christ came to earth in the form of a man. *(page 37)*

___ True   ___ False

3.   Studying the teachings of others is as good as studying the Bible for yourself. *(page 38)*

___ True   ___ False

4.   What is the goal for every woman's life? *(page 38)*

_____

For Further Study

King David was not ashamed of God – 2 Samuel 6:5, 14-16, 21-22.
A woman's identity – *"Not ... outward adornment, such as braided hair and the wearing of gold jewelry and fine clothes ... inner self, the unfading beauty of a gentle and quiet spirit, which is of great worth in God's sight"* 1 Peter 3:3, 4 NIV
God knows you more than you know yourself – Psalm 139.
The Lord has plans for you – Jeremiah 29:11.
Identify with Christ – John 12:25-26; Romans 6:4; 12:1-2; 13:14; Ephesians 4:22-24; Colossians 3:1-10; 1 Peter 2:1-3.
Christ's care for you – *"He maketh intercession for the saints"* Romans 8:27; Hebrews 9:24; *"We have an advocate with the Father, Jesus Christ the righteous"* 1 John 2:1; *"The Father himself loveth you, because ye have loved me, and have believed that I came out from God"* John 16:27.

Practical:

1. What sin do a husband and wife commit or invite into their lives when they do the following:

    a. They knowingly cheat on their income taxes, then ask God to bless their finances.

        Sin: _____

    b. They rent pornographic movies for "fun."

        Sin: _____

    c. They keep talking about the private schools their children attend.

        Sin: _____

    d. They spend each Sunday afternoon critiquing the pastor's morning message.

        Sin: _____

2. A husband and wife committed fornication before marrying. What can they do about it now?

    _____

3. How can a husband help his wife solve her identity crisis?

    _____

Repeat this prayer out loud:

Father, in Jesus' Name, I ask You to forgive me for the five sins that keep me out of my Promised Land, and I apply the Blood of Jesus to my household, to cleanse us from all our sins. Help me lead my wife in righteousness and give direction to my entire family to help them solve their identity crisis. Thank You, Amen.

Principles I want to memorize:

Self Test *Lesson 2*

1. What were the five reasons God gave as to why an entire generation wasn't able to enter Canaan?

   a. _____   d. _____

   b. _____   e. _____

   c. _____

2. Where are these sins listed in Scripture? *(give the book and chapter)*

   _____

3. Women are not subject to the same temptations to sin as men. ___ True ___ False

4. Define "lasciviousness." _____

5. Name the three basic temptations:

   a. _____

   b. _____

   c. _____

6. Give the Scriptural reference for the three basic sins. *(give the book, chapter and verse)*

   _____

7. Scripture says no one who abides in Christ can habitually _____.

8. What sin would we be guilty of if we demanded that God do something that is contrary to His Word?

   _____

9. Pornography is a form of: *(circle one)*

   a. murmuring   b. fornication   c. idolatry

10. When it comes to Christianity, _____ is the basic issue.

Keep this test for your records.

Lesson 3
Seize the Opportunity!

Lesson 3
Seize the Opportunity!

A. Read 1 Samuel 25.

   1. What did Abigail seize the opportunity to do? *(page 40)*

   _____

   _____

   2. What was Nabal described as? *(page 40)*

   a. a wise man   b. a caring soul   c. a fool

B. Write out Colossians 4:5.

   _____

   _____

   1. Women are to make the most of every opportunity. *(pages 40-41)* ___ True ___ False

   2. What are women to commit and submit to the Lord? *(circle all that apply) (page 41)*

   a. talents   b. complaints   c. desires   d. dreams   e. fears

For Further Study

Seize the opportunity – Ephesians 5:15, 16.

Examples – Rebekah in Genesis 24:55-67; David and Goliath in 1 Samuel 17; Shadrach, Meshach and Abednego in Daniel 3:8-30; Mary, the Lord's servant, in Luke 1:26-38; One criminal at the crucifixion in Luke 23:32-43 God equips and stays with those He chooses – Abraham – Genesis 15; 17:4, 19, 21; Abraham's servant – Genesis 24:1-27; Moses – Exodus 3:10-4:17; Joshua – Joshua 1:1-9; Gideon – Judges 6:11-7:25; Daniel – Daniel 6; The disciples – John 14:15-21; Saul/Paul – Acts 9:1-31; 2 Timothy 1:12.

3. Who is responsible for the intelligence, talents, abilities and gifts God has given to you? *(page 42)*

    ___ You yourself   ___ Your teachers   ___ Your spouse

4. These do need _____, however. *(fill in the blank) (page 42)*

    a. cultivation   b. toning down   c. rethinking

5. Deborah and Esther are both biblical examples of what? *(circle one) (page 43)*

    a. failures   b. overcomers   c. housewives   d. shy people

C. Christ-likeness and _____ are synonymous. *(page 45)*

1. What is the basic quality of womanhood? *(circle one) (page 45)*

    a. nagging   b. femininity   c. forcefulness   d. talking

2. What happens when women try to compete with men by copying them? *(page 45)*

    _____

    _____

3. Women can be great achievers. *(page 46)*   ___ True   ___ False

---

For Further Study

Commit, submit, seize – Psalms 21:1-7; 37:3-6; 55:22; 145:17-20; Isaiah 41:10, 13; Matthew 4:18-22; 6:31-34; Mark 10:28; Luke 5:27-28.

Train the younger women – Titus 2:3-5.

Take responsibility to cultivate and invest your God-given talents – Matthew 25:14-30; *"Do not neglect the gift which is in you"* 1 Timothy 4:14 AMP; *"Fan into flame the gift of God … Guard the good deposit that was entrusted to you"* 2 Timothy 1:6-7, 14 NIV.

Overcome – Jacob – Genesis 32:28; Father of the boy with the evil spirit – Mark 9:24; Seventy-two disciples – Luke 10:19.

Stand – 1 Corinthians 15:58; 16:13; Philippians 3:12, 14; 4:1; 1 John 4:4; 5:4, 5; Revelation 21:7-8.

The basic quality in womanhood is femininity – 1 Peter 3:1-6.

4. What are the dangers of men who hide behind a strong woman? *(pages 46-47)*

    _____

    _____

5. A strong woman can make a man _____. *(fill in the blank) (page 47)*

    a. morally lazy   b. crazy   c. better   d. happier

D. Define a "Jezebel" spirit. *(page 47)*

    _____

    _____

1. A man in ministry who has a _____ and _____ wife can do very well, as

    long as the man _____.
    (page 47)

2. Biblically, women should not be involved in ministry. *(page 47)*

    ___ True   ___ False

For Further Study

"It's harder to make amends with an offended friend than to capture a fortified city. Arguments separate friends like a gate locked with iron bars" Proverbs 18:19 NLT.

A "morally lazy" man – the wicked, lazy, worthless servant in Matthew 25:26, 30

Scripture warns against laziness – Proverbs 6:6-8; 10:4; 12:24; 24:30-34; Ecclesiastes 10:18; 1 Timothy 5:8; Hebrews 6:12.

Effects of the "Jezebel" spirit – King Ahab *"sullen and angry … lay on his bed sulking and refused to eat"* 1 Kings 21:4 NIV. Jezebel assumed the authority (vs. 7, 8), and Ahab earned the consequences (v. 19).

3.   In what ways can the principle "prayer produces intimacy" become negative? *(page 48)*

_____

_____

4.   Giftings and anointings are no substitute for: *(circle one) (page 48)*

   a. authority   b. ministry   c. obedience   d. jewelry

Practical:

1.   In the story of Abigail and Nabal, are there similarities between you and Nabal? Are there areas in your life that could be considered "foolish"? Does it force your spouse to intercede for you?

_____

_____

2.   What opportunities do women you know have which they should seize?

_____

_____

3.   Who are the women in Christ's life and the Early Church? Discuss with a friend or spouse the role of women in ministry.

_____

Repeat this prayer out loud:

Father, thank You for helping me to recognize the opportunities women around me have. Help me encourage them in their giftings and anointings. And, help me to recognize when they are doing the same for me, interceding for me to become more of a man of God. Thank You for sending such people into my life. In Christ's Name, I pray, Amen.

For Further Study

Imitate Christ's humility – Philippians 2:1-11.

Self Test *Lesson 3*

1. In what portion of Scripture do we find the story of Abigail and Nabal? *(give the book, chapter and verses)*

    _____

2. Who is responsible for a woman's intelligence, talents, abilities and gifts given to her by God?

    _____

3. Name some examples of courageous women in the Bible.

    _____   _____   _____   _____

4. What is the basic quality of womanhood? _____

5. What happens when women try to compete with men by copying them?

    _____

    _____

6. Women can be great achievers.   ___ True   ___ False

7. How is it that a strong woman can make a man morally lazy?

    _____

8. What are some of the character traits of a "Jezebel" spirit?

    _____

    _____

9. Giftings and anointings are no substitute for: *(circle one)*

    a. marriage   b. ministry   c. obedience

    Keep this test for your records.

Lesson 4

There Has to Be a Chapter on Submission

Lesson 4
There Has to Be a Chapter on Submission

A. Submission is God's plan for _____. *(fill in the blank) (page 49)*

restoration   bondage   women only

1. Mark "T" for True and "F" for False. *(pages 49-51)*

____ a. Much error is preached with regard to submission.

____ b. Error contains no elements of truth.

____ c. "Transcendent glory" means God takes what is meant for evil and turns it to our good.

____ d. The people of the plain of Shinar were rendered helpless by God breaking their arms.

____ e. God used languages to unite believers in the Early Church.

____ f. The agreement of believers results in power.

____ g. Adam and Eve were never equal from the beginning.

____ h. Submission was part of the curse but now elevates women to joint-heirship.

____ i. When done right, submission requires no faith.

____ j. A woman's submission to her husband illustrates her submission to the Lord.

____ k. If a husband does not treat his wife as a joint-heir, his prayers won't get ready answers.

For Further Study

Waiting on the Lord – *"Wait for the promise of the Father"* Acts 1:4; Psalms 27:14; 33:20; 130:5, 6; Isaiah 8:17; 30:18.
Christ's relationship with the Church – Ephesians 5:21-33; Colossians 3:19
The husband's responsibilities – *"Likewise, ye husbands, dwell with them according to knowledge, giving honour unto the wife, as unto the weaker vessel, and as being heirs together of the grace of life; that your prayers be not hindered"* 1 Peter 3:7; *"You husbands must be careful of your wives, being thoughtful of their needs and honoring them as the weaker sex … you and your wife are partners in receiving God's blessings, and if you don't treat her as you should, your prayers will not get ready answers"* 1 Peter 3:7 TLB; *"Husbands, love your wives and be not bitter against them"* Colossians 3:19; *"Live joyfully with the wife whom thou lovest all the days of the life of thy vanity"* Ecclesiastes 9:9.

2. What happens when a woman voluntarily submits to her husband? *(page 51)*

_____

_____

3. The husband of a rebellious wife may resort to: *(page 51)*

___ ruling   ___ leading

B. Write out 1 Peter 3:7. _____

_____

_____

1. What is the danger of "office wives"? *(circle one) (page 52)*

    a. too much intimacy   b. too much efficiency   c. too much nagging

2. Read aloud Hebrews 4:12.

3. The Word of God is necessary to discover your own _____. *(page 52)*

    a. problems   b. motives   c. weaknesses

For Further Study

God won't hear those holding iniquity in their heart – Deuteronomy 1:43-46; 1 Samuel 8:18-20; James 4:3; 1 John 3:21-23; 5:14.

Contentious wives – *"It is better to dwell in a corner of the housetop [on the flat oriental roof, exposed to all kinds of weather] than in a house shared with a nagging, quarrelsome, and faultfinding woman"* Proverbs 21:9 AMP; *"It is better to live alone in the corner of an attic than with a contentious wife in a lovely home"* Proverbs 25:24 NLT.

The wise woman – Proverbs 14:1

The Lord's wisdom is available – 1 Kings 3:9-12; Proverbs 2:1-11; Daniel 1:17; 2:21b; Matthew 7:7.

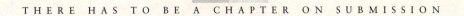
C. What are the two most frequently asked questions by women? *(page 53)*

1. _____

2. _____

Author's Note: Since the first publication of this book, these questions have been eclipsed by a third, which is, "What can I do about my husband's addiction to pornography?"

D. Read Ephesians 5:21-33 and 1 Peter 3:1.

Would these be contrary to your nature?   ___ Yes ___ No

Are they contrary to your wife's nature?   ___ Yes ___ No

For Further Study

Submit to one another – *"You wives must remember that your husbands might be converted because of you. And you husbands must remember that your wives might be converted because of you"* 1 Corinthians 7:16 NLT.
Submission – 1 Corinthians 9:19, 22-24; Romans 15:1, 2; 1 Thessalonians 5:14; 1 Peter 4:8
Seek good for others – 1 Corinthians 10:24, 33b, c; 13:4-7; Ephesians 4:2, 3.
Trust God and His transcendent glory – Proverbs 23:18; Jeremiah 29:11; 1 Corinthians 1:9; Ephesians 1:11.

E. Mark "T" for True and "F" for False for these sentences which each begin with "Submission is ..." *(pages 54-56)*

    ____   1. the Word of God in action.

    ____   2. just a word for women.

    ____   3. a principle of business, government and school.

    ____   4. common in nature and physical life.

    ____   5. an outward action, not a matter of the heart.

    ____   6. to be prevalent in both men and women.

    ____   7. something that requires humility.

    ____   8. a wife's greatest calling.

    ____   9. a way to avoid personal responsibility.

    ____   10. a form of hiding.

    ____   11. done best by someone with a strong spirit.

    ____   12. something that reveals wisdom.

F. Define "common courtesy." *(page 56)*

1. Are husbands and wives supposed to submit their decisions to each other? *(page 57)*

    ___ Yes   ___ No

For Further Study

Love and submission are for everyone – "*Submitting yourselves one to another in the fear of God. Wives, submit yourselves unto your own husbands, as unto the Lord ... Husbands, love your wives, even as Christ also loved the church, and gave himself for it ... So ought men to love their wives as their own bodies. He that loveth his wife loveth himself. For no man ever yet hated his own flesh; but nourisheth and cherisheth it, even as the Lord the church ... Nevertheless let every one of you in particular so love his wife even as himself; and the wife see that she reverence her husband*" Ephesians 5:21, 22, 25, 28, 29, 33.

2.   What led Abraham to greatness? *(page 57)*

_____

3.   What is the wife of an unsaved husband to do? *(page 59)*

_____

_____

4.   What is developed by submission? *(page 60)* _____

Practical:

1.   Define "transcendent glory."

_____

Give a personal example:

_____

2.   Read 1 Peter 3:7. Whom do you know who does not regularly receive answers to prayer? Can it be due to his treatment of his wife?

_____

For Further Study

Submit to see change – *"Likewise, ye wives, be in subjection to your own husbands; that, if any obey not the word, they also may without the word be won by the conversation of the wives; While they behold your chaste conversation … For after this manner in the old time the holy women also, who trusted in God, adorned themselves, being in subjection unto their own husbands … Likewise, ye husbands, dwell with them according to knowledge, giving honour unto the wife, as unto the weaker vessel, and as being heirs together of the grace of life"* 1 Peter 3:1, 2, 5, 7; *"Submit yourselves to every ordinance of man for the Lord's sake … For so is the will of God, that with well doing ye may put to silence the ignorance of foolish men … Honour all men. Love the brotherhood. Fear God. Honour the king. Servants, be subject to your masters"* 1 Peter 2:13, 15, 17, 18.

3. In what ways have you made sure you earned your wife's respect and willingness to submit?

_____

4. In the Old Testament and in many cultures, men's wealth was/is measured by the number of his wives. Compare this to "office wives." What can a man do to stay pure of adulterous thoughts or actions?

_____

_____

Repeat this prayer out loud:

Father, I ask You humbly to forgive me for any arrogance I have concerning submission. Forgive me for not submitting myself to You and others, as I forgive those who do not submit to me. Help me to see others' perspectives and to become worthy of their submission and respect. In Jesus' Name, I pray, Amen.

For Further Study

Ways to earn respect – *"Husbands, in the same way be considerate as you live with your wives, and treat them with respect"* 1 Peter 3:7 NIV; *"And, ye fathers, provoke not your children to wrath: but bring them up in the nurture and admonition of the Lord"* Ephesians 6:4; *"Let us not love in word, neither in tongue, but in deed and in truth"* 1 John 3:18; *"A false witness must be punished; an honest witness is safe"* Proverbs 21:28 TLB.

Self Test *Lesson 4*

1. God's plan of restoration always includes submission.   ___ True ___ False

2. What term do we use to describe God's ability to take things meant for evil and convert them to work for our good?

    _____

3. Often, rebellion has caused some husbands to resort to _____, not _____.

4. What can cause a man to "not get ready answers" to his prayers?

    _____

5. Give the Scriptural reference for this truth. *(book, chapter and verse)*

    _____

6. The Bible teaches male dictatorship.   ___ True ___ False

7. According to Ephesians 5, wives are to submit to their husbands. How does the same chapter tell men to love their wives?

    _____

8. Submission should be used at times to avoid responsibility.   ___ True ___ False

9. Women being sexually or physically abused must continue to submit entirely to their husbands.

    ___ True ___ False

10. What does submission for a woman require? *(circle all that apply)*

    a. humility   b. faith   c. discernment   d. wisdom

Keep this test for your records.

Lesson 5

The Truth About Forgiveness

Lesson 5

The Truth About Forgiveness

A. Sometimes one needs to learn how to submit to love. *(page 61)*

___ True   ___ False

1. With what do we often associate our image of God? *(page 62)*

   a. our idea of deity   b. our own self image   c. our earthly father

2. Draw a line between the image of God and the person(s) who saw Him in that way. *(page 63)*

   a. Christ transfigured   Ezekiel
   b. Cloud by day and fire by night   Daniel
   c. Burning bush   Peter, James and John
   d. Dazzling like fire   Moses
   e. Ancient of Days   Israelites

3. Who is God to us? *(circle all that apply) (page 63)*

   a. a good man   d. stingy father
   b. All-powerful and All-knowing e. Savior of our souls
   c. Majestic Ruler of the Universe f. ruthless authoritarian

For Further Study

Knowing Who God is – Genesis 32:30; Exodus 24:10; 33:23; Numbers 12:8a; Judges 6:22; 13:22; Isaiah 6:5; *"I had heard of You [only] by the hearing of the ear, but now my [spiritual] eye sees You"* Job 42:5 AMP; *"I had heard about you before, but now I have seen you with my own eyes"* Job 42:5 NLT.
God is constant – Psalm 118:6, 7; Matthew 28:20; Hebrews 13:5.
God knows us – Psalm 139.

4. Fill in each blank using the following words: *(page 63)*

    ahead   healed   forgive   forgetting   reaching

    When you submit to God's love, you are _____ to love others and

    _____ past hurts, _____ those things which are behind

    and _____ toward those things which are _____.

5. Forgiveness is the key to breaking what? *(page 63)*

    _____

    _____

B. Christianity is not built on _____. *(fill in the blank) (page 63)*

    confession   repression   suppression

    1. Write out John 20:22-23. _____

        _____

        _____

        _____

    2. What is the right of every believer? *(page 64)*

        _____

        _____

For Further Study

God does more than we ask or think – 1 Kings 3:7-14; Romans 16:25; 2 Corinthians 9:8; Philippians 4:19; Jude 24.
God's love and ours – 1 John 4:7-21
Forgiveness – Psalm 103:8-13; Micah 7:18, 19; Romans 4:7, 8; *"Blessed is he whose transgressions are forgiven, whose sins are covered"* Psalm 32:1-7 NIV.

3. If we forgive sins, they are forgiven. *(page 64)* ___ True ___ False

4. If we do not forgive sins, they are kept. *(page 64)* ___ True ___ False

5. Forgiving others is optional. *(page 64)* ___ True ___ False

6. To forgive as God forgives requires the Holy Spirit. *(page 64)* ___ True ___ False

C. Name an instance in which a person may need to "forgive" God. *(page 65)*

_____

1. Fill in the blanks with words from the following list: *(page 66)*

    grace   mercy   love   forgiveness   holiness

    _____ is the essence of _____; mercy is the essence of

    _____; _____ is the essence of _____; and love is the essence

    of _____.

2. Can true forgiveness be earned? *(page 67)* ___ Yes ___ No

3. What happens to others when we forgive them? *(page 68)*

    _____

For Further Study

God forgives then forgets our sins – Psalms 32:1, 2; 85:2; 103:12; Isaiah 43:25; Romans 4:7, 8.
God gave us the *"ministry of reconciliation"* and committed to us the *"message of reconciliation"*
2 Corinthians 5:16-21 NIV; Matthew 5:7.
God forgives us as we forgive others – James 2:13. The Parable of the Unmerciful Servant – Matthew 18:21-35;
"Be ye therefore merciful, as your Father is also merciful. Judge not, and ye shall not be judged: condemn not, and ye shall not be condemned: forgive, and ye shall be forgiven: Give, and it shall be given unto you; good measure, pressed down, and shaken together, and running over, shall men give into your bosom. For with the same measure that ye mete withal it shall be measured to you again" Luke 6:36-38.

D. Underline every mention of forgiveness in the following passage:
Read: *"And whenever you stand praying, if you have anything against anyone, forgive him and let it drop (leave it, let it go), in order that your Father Who is in heaven may also forgive you your [own] failings and shortcomings and let them drop. But if you do not forgive, neither will your Father in heaven forgive your failings and shortcomings"* Mark 11:25-26 AMP.

1. What is important to do after forgiveness? *(circle one) (page 68)*

   a. call your pastor   b. let go   c. tell the person whom you forgave

2. What is the result of forgiveness? *(circle all that apply) (page 71)*

   a. peace of heart   b. healthiness of spirit   c. freedom of thought

Practical:

1. Why can we say that "true holiness is manifested in real forgiveness"? *(page 66)*

   _____

   _____

2. Discuss with a friend or spouse instances in which it would be detrimental and hurtful to tell a person you forgave him/her.

Repeat this prayer out loud:

Father, I come to You now, in the Name of Jesus. By faith, I ask You to forgive me and cleanse me of all my sins. You said unless I forgive, You would not forgive me. So right now I ask You to forgive me and cleanse my heart and mind of all sin. By faith, I receive the power of the Holy Spirit into my life. By the ability of Your Spirit and the authority of Your Word, I forgive the person who has sinned against me. I release his/her sin out of my life. Thank You, Lord, for what You are doing to make me free from my own sin and the sins of others. Amen.

For Further Study

When you forgive, release – John 20:22; 2 Corinthians 10:4, 5; James 3:17, 18.
Forgiveness is in word and spirit – *"This is how my heavenly Father will treat each of you unless you forgive your brother from your heart"* Matthew 18:35; Psalm 49:7, 8; Ephesians 1:7; 2:8-9.
Be free – Ephesians 6:10-18; James 4:7; 1 Peter 5:6-10.

Self Test *Lesson 5*

1. Some women need to learn how to submit to love. ___ True ___ False

2. What image is often confused with our image of God? _____

3. Can forgiveness be the key to break the cycle of sins passed from one generation to another?

   ___ Yes ___ No

   Explain your answer.

   _____

   _____

4. Christianity is built upon: *(circle one)*

   a. suppression   b. confession   c. repression

5. In what passage of Scripture can you find the principle of "release"? *(give book, chapter and verses)*

   _____

6. How is it possible to retain the sins of others? _____

7. Forgiving others is optional. ___ True ___ False

8. To forgive as God forgives requires the Holy Spirit. ___ True ___ False

9. It is blasphemous to think a person could need to "forgive" God. ___ True ___ False

10. Is it possible to be full of good works, have all the outward expression of holiness and still have an evil heart?

    ___ Yes ___ No

11. Forgiveness is never earned but is always a free gift. ___ True ___ False

Keep this test for your records.

Lesson 6

The Power of Sex

Lesson 6
The Power of Sex

A.   Sex is meant for _____. *(fill in the blank) (page 73)*

good   pleasure   reproduction

1.   Sex is an expression of, not a means to achieve _____. *(page 74)*

2.   What is a good "self-assessment" as to our own attitudes towards sex? *(page 74)*

_____

_____

B.   What effect can unforgiveness and bitterness have on sexual fulfillment? *(circle one) (page 75)*

hinder   no effect   enhance

1.   What is the answer to good, healthy sex? *(circle all that apply) (page 75)*

a. fidelity in marriage

b. pornographic foreplay

c. abstinence outside marriage

For Further Study
God has good purposes for sex – Genesis 1:27, 28, 31; Malachi 2:15; Matthew 19:4, 5.
The world has perverted sex – Romans 1:24; The Church must correct the perversion – Malachi 2:7.
Sex is honorable – Hebrews 13:4; *"Every good gift and every perfect gift is from above, and cometh down from the Father of lights, with whom is no variableness, neither shadow of turning"* James 1:17.
God's covenant plan – Genesis 17:10; Romans 2:29; 4:3
Guard against anger, unforgiveness and bitterness, which can hinder sexual fulfillment – Psalm 4:4;
2 Corinthians 2:10, 11; Ephesians 4:26.

2.   Consistent times of prayer together produce what for a husband and wife? *(page 76)*

___ sexual fulfillment   ___ antagonistic attitudes

3.   Read: *"But the man who has doubts (misgivings, an uneasy conscience) ... stands condemned [before God], because he does not act from faith. For whatever does not originate and proceed from faith is sin [whatever is done without a conviction of its approval by God is sinful]"* Romans 14:23 AMP.

In what way does this passage relate to our sexuality? _____

_____

_____

_____

C.   Sex is _____. *(fill in the blank) (page 79)*

sacred   an abomination   something not to discuss in Christianity

For Further Study

God wants to be glorified in marriage – Ephesians 5:25; *"Whatsoever ye do, do all to the glory of God"* 1 Corinthians 10:31; Matthew 5:16; *"Christ in you, the hope of glory"* Colossians 1:27.
Stay pure – *"Do not conform any longer to the pattern of this world"* Romans 12:2 NIV; Ephesians 4:17-19, 22-24; 1 Peter 1:14, 22; 1 John 2:15-17; *"Wherewithall shall a young man cleanse his way? by taking heed thereto according to thy word"* Psalm 119:9; John 17:17; *"You are already clean because of the word I have spoken to you"* John 15:3 NIV.

D. Match the covenant with its external sign by placing the correct letter next to its number. *(page 79)*

   ____ 1. Marriage covenant   a. circumcision

   ____ 2. Christianity's covenant   b. sex

   ____ 3. Abraham's covenant   c. baptism and communion

E. Write out Hebrews 13:4.

_____

_____

1. Sex was made for _____. *(fill in the blank) (page 79)*

   a. lusting and getting   b. grasping and exploiting   c. loving and giving

2. What does lust do? *(page 79)*   ___ Limits   ___ Releases

3. What does love do? *(page 79)*   ___ Limits   ___ Releases

4. What did God make sex? *(page 80)*   ___ Good   ___ Bad

5. What does sin make sex? *(page 80)*   ___ Good   ___ Bad

6. Who holds the "power of sex"? *(circle one) (page 80)*

   a. women   b. men   c. God   d. the world

For Further Study

Marriage is a covenant – *"Therefore shall a man leave his father and his mother, and shall cleave unto his wife: and they shall be one flesh"* Genesis 2:24; *"Yet is she thy companion, and the wife of thy covenant"* Malachi 2:14; *"You were united to your wife by the Lord. In God's wise plan, when you married, the two of you became one person in his sight ... Keep faith with the wife of your youth"* Malachi 2:15 TLB; Malachi 2:15; Romans 7:2; *"The man should give his wife all that is her right as a married woman, and the wife should do the same for the husband"* 1 Corinthians 7:3 TLB; *"Honor your marriage and its vows, and be pure; for God will surely punish all those who are immoral or commit adultery"* Hebrews 13:4 TLB.

Lust limits; love releases – *"The words of the Lord Jesus, how he said, It is more blessed to give than to receive"* Acts 20:35; John 10:10, 15:13; Romans 12:9, 10; 1 Corinthians 13:4-7; Ephesians 5:25; 2 Timothy 3:2; Hebrews 13:4; James 4:1-3; 1 Peter 4:8-10.

F.   Woman was created to be the _____ of a man. *(fill in the blank) (page 80)*

completer   competitor   conscience

1.   In what way can women "defile" a marriage bed? *(circle one) (page 81)*

a. use it as blackmail   b. enjoy sex   c. compete for sexual favors

G.   Educating the young concerning sex is whose responsibility? *(circle all that apply) (page 82)*

a. Church   b. parents   c. school counselors   d. movies

1.   How can we stop AIDS? *(circle all that apply) (page 82)*

a. give children condoms   b. educate children about safe sex   c. teach virginity

2.   We should teach only what is wrong with sexual immorality. *(page 83)*

___ True   ___ False

3.   There is a positive aspect to sexual purity. *(page 83)*

___ True   ___ False

For Further Study

Teach and train – *"Impress them on your children"* Deuteronomy 6:5-9 NIV; *"Teach them to your children"* Deuteronomy 11:18-21 NIV; Ephesians 6:4; Colossians 3:16; 1 Thessalonians 4:1-8.
What to teach – *"Set an example ... in speech, in life, in love, in faith and in purity"* 1 Timothy 4:11-13 NIV; Titus 2:2-8.
Who should teach – Fathers and mothers – Proverbs 1:8, 9; 4:1; 6:20-24 NIV; Spiritual leaders – Malachi 2:7 NIV; The righteous – Proverbs 10:21 NIV; Elders – 1 Timothy 1:18; 4:14 NIV

H. How can a dominant husband be defeated in bed? *(page 83)*

_____

What is wrong with a woman's "holier-than-thou, don't touch me" attitude? *(page 84)*

_____

Practical:

1. In your opinion, what purpose does the book "Song of Solomon" serve?

    _____

2. Why is it important for a husband and wife to learn each other's preferences in sex?

    _____

3. In what way does the woman, not the man, have the power of sex? Why do you think this is so?

    _____

For Further Study

Enjoy God's creation – *"My beloved is mine and I am his"* Song of Solomon 2:16.

4.   Discuss with a friend or spouse the stereotype of a "good" and "bad" woman? In what ways have you succumbed to believing a false image? Can "good" women enjoy sex?

_____

5.   Read Romans 2:21-24. What has happened to the Church as a result of clergy immorality?

_____

6.   Name some practical reasons not to engage in pornography.

_____

Repeat this prayer out loud:

Father, in Jesus' Name, please forgive me for sexual sins—those I've committed and those I've thought about. Please purify me (and my wife) in this area of our lives and make our sex life a glory to You! Amen.

Principles I want to memorize:

Self Test *Lesson 6*

1. The Bible speaks of anything sexual as intrinsically evil.   ___ True   ___ False

2. Sex is to be based on the desire to give, not to get.   ___ True   ___ False

3. What effect can unforgiveness and bitterness have on sexual fulfillment? *(circle one)*

   a. hinder   b. no effect   c. enhance

4. Name at least two ways to achieve good, healthy sex.

   a. _____

   b. _____

5. Sex is an external evidence of what? _____

6. Woman was created to be man's: *(circle one)*

   a. completer   b. competitor   c. predator

7. What does lust do?   ___ Limits   ___ Releases

8. It is the sole responsibility of the parents to educate their children regarding sex.

   ___ True   ___ False

9. Name at least one myth about sexual fulfillment.

   _____

10. In your opinion, what will sexual "put-downs" do to either partner in a marriage?

    _____

    _____

Keep this test for your records.

Lesson 7
Myths of Marriage

Lesson 7
Myths of Marriage

A. What is life's greatest teacher? *(page 87)* _____

   1. What must be experienced in order to know the joy of salvation? *(circle one) (page 87)*

      a. bondage to sin   b. a bad background   c. the sorrow of repentance

   2. Read John 16:21, Ecclesiastes 7:3 and 2 Corinthians 7:10.

      Write out the principle these illustrate. *(page 87)*

      _____

      _____

B. List in order the two most important decisions you'll ever make. *(pages 87-88)*

   1. _____

   2. _____

For Further Study
Joy is birthed out of sorrow – Esther 9:22; Psalms 30:5, 11; 126:5, 6; Jeremiah 31:9-17; John 16:20; *"Now I rejoice, not that ye were made sorry, but that ye sorrowed to repentance: for ye were made sorry after a godly manner"* 2 Corinthians 7:9.
Make a decision – The double-minded waver between right and wrong because they are undecided – 1 Kings 18:21. They profess to hate sin, but have a lingering love for it – James 4:1.
They do not have a right understanding of good and evil – Hebrews 5:14.

C. Mark "T" for True and "F" for False. *(pages 88-89)*

____ 1. Christian women are the most attractive on earth.

____ 2. As a Christian woman seeks God, men will seek her.

____ 3. New construction is always harder than reconstruction.

____ 4. The only constant in maturity is change.

____ 5. Truth does not vary, but the way we apply it can change.

____ 6. Expectations of marriage must stay the same decade after decade.

____ 7. Most women work outside the home.

____ 8. Most women earn more money than their husbands.

____ 9. Most women have less leisure time than men.

For Further Study

Men are attracted to godly women – *"Esther won the favor of everyone who saw her"* including King Xerxes – Esther 2:15-17 NIV; *"All my fellow townsmen know that you are a woman of noble character"* Ruth 3:11 NIV. A woman's beauty – 1 Peter 3:3-5

D. Life is where you find it and _____. *(page 90)*

1. Since Jesus Christ is the same yesterday, today and tomorrow, can His message be preached in the same pastoral setting as the Early Church? *(page 90)*

    ___ Yes ___ No

2. Are the principles Jesus gave us timeless? *(page 90)*   ___ Yes ___ No

3. Time management is needed in: *(circle all that apply)* *(page 90)*

    a. a household   b. industry   c. big business

E. What is a great danger for a single woman contemplating marriage? *(page 91)*

    _____

1. God is a: *(page 91)*   ___ magician   ___ miracle worker

2. Which of the following sets are synonymous? *(circle one)* *(page 91)*

    a. truth and positive thinking   b. images and reality   c. truth and reality

3. Why is Jesus the ultimate reality? *(circle all that apply)* *(page 91)*

    a. He is Truth.   b. He is fully God.   c. He is fully human.

For Further Study

Godly principles are relevant – Numbers 23:19; Psalms 9:7-10; 90:1, 2; 102:24-28; 136; Malachi 3:6, 7; James 1:17; *"The secret things belong unto the Lord our God: but those things which are revealed belong unto us and to our children for ever, that we may do all the words of this law"* Deuteronomy 29:29.
Godly management – Luke 16:1-12; 1 Corinthians 4:1, 2; *"One that ruleth well his own house"* 1 Timothy 3:4 NIV (also vs. 1-5, 12); *"I will therefore that the younger women marry, bear children, guide the house"* 1 Timothy 5:14; Titus 1:6-7.

4.   Fill in the following sentences with words from the list below: *(page 92)*

character   before   after   personality

When a woman marries, she marries the _____ of the man, not

his _____. That's why whatever a man is _____

marriage, he will be more of _____ marriage.

F.   *"I have some misgivings, but _____."* *(page 93)*

1.   It's dangerous to go against your _____. *(fill in) (page 93)*

a. fiance's wishes   b. better judgment   c. mother-in-law

2.   Read Philippians 4:7.

G.   *"I can change him _____."* *(page 94)*

1.   Husbands are not given to women as: *(circle one) (page 94)*

a. construction projects   b. providers   c. protectors

2.   If a man doesn't meet a woman's needs before marriage, he won't after. *(page 94)*

___ True   ___ False

For Further Study

Choose a good name – *"A good name is better than fine perfume"* Ecclesiastes 7:1 NIV; *"A good name is rather to be chosen than great riches, and loving favour rather than silver and gold"* Proverbs 22:1.
Choose character – Proverbs 31:23, 30, 31.
Find the peace of God – Psalms 22:5; 28:7; 85:8; Isaiah 12:2; 26:3; John 14:27; 16:33; *"And let the peace of God rule in your hearts, to the which also ye are called in one body; and be ye thankful"* Colossians 3:15.

H. *"I do not need an _____ because we will be married forever, and he will provide for me." (page 94)*

Did the "Proverbs 31" woman work outside the home?   ___ Yes   ___ No

I. Men are smarter than women. *(page 95)*   ___ True ___ False

Define the term "Cinderella Syndrome." *(page 95)*

_____

_____

J. *"My most important goal is _____."*
    (page 95)

Every individual, male or female, must know that if they are not happy single, _____

_____. *(page 96)*

For Further Study

Women working outside the home – Proverbs 31; Acts 16:14, 15, 40

Prepared as singles for love – Isaac and Rebekah in Genesis 24

A good name – *"Whoever heard me spoke well of me"* Job 29:11 NIV (also vs. 7-17).

A bad name – *"that wicked man Nabal. He is just like his name—his name is Fool"* 1 Samuel 25:25 NIV.

Practical:

1. Read Proverbs 22:1. Do you provide your family with a "good name"? Are they proud to be known as yours?

    _____

2. Either purposefully or accidentally, did your wife marry a construction project? Are you progressing?

    _____

3. Discuss what thoughts this chapter has given you about how you instruct your children regarding marriage.

    _____

Repeat this prayer out loud:

Father, in Jesus' Name, I thank You for my (future) spouse and I pray that You will "maximize" all the unique talents and abilities You have given to her. I release her, by faith, to pursue all that You have for her. Amen.

Principles I want to memorize:

Self Test *Lesson 7*

1. Name at least two areas of life that illustrate the principle that "all true joy is born out of sorrow."

    _____

    _____

2. The most important decision you'll ever make is whom you marry.   ___ True ___ False

3. Why does a single woman of good Christian character particularly need to be careful?

    _____

    _____

4. New construction is always harder than reconstruction.   ___ True ___ False

5. Truth does not vary, but expectations about life do.   ___ True ___ False

6. God is a: ___ magician   ___ miracle worker

7. Facing reality is: *(circle one)*

    a. the worst way to live   b. a boring way to live   c. the only way to live

8. Name at least two myths women may believe about marriage:

    a. _____

    b. _____

Keep this test for your records.

Lesson 8
The "Merge Crisis"

Lesson 8
The "Merge Crisis"

A. Name the two basic activities in life. *(page 99)*

1. _____   2. _____

B. Name the four basic desires we all seek to satisfy. *(page 99)*

1. _____   2. _____   3. _____   4. _____

C. _____ requires the merging of two into one. *(fill in the blank) (page 99)*

Blending   Belonging   Believing

1. What must a man do when a woman merges her identity into his? *(circle one) (page 100)*

a. give her a character she is pleased to identify with
b. make her submit to him
c. merge his identity into hers

2. Read Ephesians 5:25.

3. What must a man provide his wife which Christ provides the Church? *(page 100)*

a. _____   b. _____   c. _____

For Further Study

Choices – *"I will go"* Genesis 24:58; *"Choose you this day whom ye will serve"* Joshua 24:15; *"When Naomi realized that Ruth was determined"* Ruth 1:15-18 NIV; *"How long will you waver between two opinions"* 1 Kings 18:21 NIV; *"Be it known unto thee, O king, that we will not serve thy gods, nor worship the golden image which thou hast set up"* Daniel 3:18; *"I press toward the mark"* Philippians 3:14 (also vs. 12-21).
Merging – Malachi 2:15; Matthew 19:5, 6; Mark 10:7, 8; Ephesians 5:31
A man's love – Ephesians 5:28, 29; Colossians 3:19

4.   What is necessary to keep from breaking resolutions? *(page 100)*

a. revelation   b. strict discipline   c. innocence

5.   We have a tendency to judge: *(circle one) (page 100)*

a. ourselves by our emotions, others by their motions.
b. ourselves by our intentions, others by their actions.
c. ourselves harshly, others leniently.

D.   A woman dreams of a man in terms of the ideal, then marries the _____.
(fill in the blank) (page 100)

wrong man   phony   real   slob

1.   Disappointments in life are based on _____. *(page 100)*

a. how bad things get   b. what we find   c. what we expected to find

2.   What gap needs to be closed for a woman to "merge" successfully in marriage? *(page 100)*

_____

For Further Study

Judging others – Matthew 7:1-5; Luke 6:37-38; Romans 14:4, 10, 13; 1 Corinthians 4:3-5
Intentions vs. actions – Proverbs 21:8; Romans 2:13; James 1:22-25; *"Having therefore these promises, dearly beloved, let us cleanse ourselves from all filthiness of the flesh and spirit, perfecting holiness in the fear of God"* 2 Corinthians 7:1.
Ideal – *"Don't let anyone think little of you because you are young. Be their ideal; let them follow the way you teach and live; be a pattern for them in your love, your faith, and your clean thoughts"* 1 Timothy 4:12 TLB.

3. Why don't people discuss the most important things in life? *(circle all that apply)* *(pages 100-101)*

    a. they're the most intimate

    b. it requires "dying to self"

    c. you have to kill pride

    d. it is painful

    e. you have to share likes and dislikes

    f. you have to admit weaknesses

    g. you have to deal with truth

    h. you have to kill the person after you tell him

E. Name three things that Christ is for you. *(page 101)*

1. _____   2. _____   3. _____

Marriage is an _____ in which _____ your own portrait. *(page 101)*

For Further Study

Truth – *"Know the truth"* John 8:32; *"The Spirit of truth … will guide you into all truth"* John 16:13 NIV.
Christ indwells us – *"Let the peace of Christ rule in your hearts … Let the word of Christ dwell in you richly"*
Colossians 3:15, 16 NIV.
Mediator, Counselor, Reconciler – John 14:16, 26; 15:26 NIV; Romans 5:10, 11 NIV; Ephesians 1:10; 2:13;
Hebrews 12:24 NIV

F. Write in the letter of the phrase on the right which correctly completes the sentence. *(pages 101-102)*

____ 1. Maturation is
a. temporary period of pressurized time

____ 2. Most marriages begin in
b. immaturity

____ 3. Maturity requires
c. men

____ 4. Selfishness is a trait of
d. devastatingly selfish

____ 5. Women who refuse to "merge" can be
e. immature childishness

____ 6. Crisis is a
f. commitment

____ 7. Jezebel was
g. devilish in motives and actions

____ 8. Women have power with
h. a lifelong process

G. Read about Jezebel in 1 Kings 18-19, 21 and 2 Kings 9:30-37.
Read about Potiphar's wife in Genesis 39:7-20.

Name a similarity between Potiphar's wife and Jezebel.

_____

For Further Study

Maturation is a lifelong process – *"You, therefore, must be perfect [growing into complete maturity of godliness in mind and character, having reached the proper height of virtue and integrity], as your heavenly Father is perfect"* Matthew 5:48 AMP; *"We also rejoice in our sufferings, because we know that suffering produces perseverance; perseverance, character; and character, hope"* Romans 5:3-5 NIV; Romans 8:37; Galatians 6:9.

1. Define a "Jezebel" spirit. *(pages 102-103)* _____

    _____

2. Name the steps in the process of destruction. *(page 103)*

    a. Deception

    b. _____

    c. Dislocation

    d. _____

H. Complete the following sentences using the words provided. *(pages 105-106)*

    permanent   hiding   crisis

    1. Even in a godly marriage _____ is normal to life.

    2. God takes us from the transient by crisis to bring us to the _____.

    3. Women who put all the responsibility on their husband's shoulders are actually involved in a

        form of _____, not submission.

For Further Study

Jezebel spirit example – Herodias manipulated her daughter and her husband, King Herod, to kill John the Baptist – Mark 6:17-28.

A worthy, noble, wise woman – Proverbs 14:1; 18:22; 19:14; 24:3, 4; 1 Corinthians 11:7

Persevere to mature – *"Let us not become weary in doing good, for at the proper time we will reap a harvest if we do not give up"* Galatians 6:9 NIV; 1 Corinthians 15:58; 2 Thessalonians 3:13; 1 Timothy 4:16; Hebrews 12:1-3.

Develop a forgiving spirit – Romans 12:16; 1 Corinthians 1:10; Ephesians 4:3; Colossians 3:14.

Practical:

1. Why must men beware the "Jezebel" spirit?

    _____

2. How might a woman act who is guilty of being a "Jezebel"?

    _____

3. How might a woman act who is not?

    _____

4. How would a man know the difference between the two?

    _____

Repeat this prayer out loud:

Father, I thank You for teaching me about women! Thank You for giving me understanding and insight. Help me aid my (future) spouse through her "merge crisis" and provide the kind of identity that is pleasing to You as well as to her. In Christ's Name, I pray, Amen.

Principles I want to memorize:

Self Test *Lesson 8*

1. What are the four basic desires we all seek to satisfy?

    a. _____

    b. _____

    c. _____

    d. _____

2. We have a tendency to judge others by their _____ but ourselves by our _____.

3. A woman tends to dream of a man in terms of the: *(circle one)*

    a. unreal   b. ideal   c. free meal

4. Name some reasons why it is difficult to discuss the most important things in life.

    _____

    _____

5. Maturation is a lifelong process.   ___ True ___ False

6. Selfishness is a trait of immaturity.   ___ True ___ False

7. Women can refuse to merge if they don't want to.   ___ True ___ False

8. Crisis is normal to life.   ___ True ___ False

9. If God truly joins two people together in marriage, they will have little or no problems.

    ___ True ___ False

Keep this test for your records.

Lesson 9

Helpmeet or Hindrance?

Lesson 9

Helpmeet or Hindrance?

A. Men and Women: Different!

1. Men feel   ___ threatened   ___ guilty

2. Women feel   ___ threatened   ___ guilty

3. Women tend to give   ___ ultimatums   ___ accusations

4. Men tend to make   ___ ultimatums   ___ accusations

5. Women want a man to be   ___ a man   ___ a woman

6. Men want a woman to be   ___ a man   ___ a woman

B. What is one of the hardest things for a man to do? *(circle one)* *(page 109)*

golf   admit he's wrong   ask for directions

For Further Study

The differences bring unity – Genesis 2:24. *"In the Lord, however, woman is not independent of man, nor is man independent of woman"* 1 Corinthians 11:11 NIV.

Women can misuse power – King David's wife Michal – 2 Samuel 6:16, 20-23; *"The contentions of a wife are a continual dropping"* Proverbs 19:13; *"It is better to dwell in the wilderness, than with a contentious and an angry woman"* Proverbs 21:19; Proverbs 25:24.

1. What is one of the hardest things for a woman to do? *(circle one) (page 109)*

   a. allow her man to fail   b. be quiet   c. kill a spider

2. Wives need to learn to accept their husbands when: *(circle all that apply) (page 109)*

   a. he makes wrong decisions   b. he's failed   c. he's weak   d. he's wrong

3. What precedes success? *(page 109)*

   _____

4. What must be done to achieve the glory of resurrection? *(page 109)*

   _____

5. To whom do men belong? *(circle one) (page 109)*

   a. the team   b. their wives   c. their employer   d. their mother   e. God

6. Men are stewards of _____. *(page 109)*

7. Women are stewards of _____. *(page 109)*

For Further Study

Sarah's faith – Genesis 12:13; 20:2; *"The holy women of the past who put their hope in God … submissive to their own husbands, like Sarah, who obeyed Abraham and called him her master"* 1 Peter 3:5, 6 NIV.
Failure precedes success – 1 Samuel 30:1-20; 2 Samuel 2:4; *"But David found strength in the Lord his God"* 1 Samuel 30:6 NIV.

C.   Besides wanting a husband to change, a woman must desire change for whom? *(page 109)*

_____

1.   What happens when women don't realize "only God can change a man's nature"? *(page 110)*

_____

2.   What helps a man who is in transition with his profession? *(page 110)*

_____

3.   To make changes, women must have faith in: *(circle one) (page 111)*

a. both God and their husbands   b. God and themselves   c. the future

D.   Being a helpmeet implies _____. *(fill in the blank) (page 112)*

giving   taking   becoming a doormat

1.   Being a hindrance implies _____. *(fill in the blank) (page 112)*

giving   taking   becoming a doormat

For Further Study

Be willing to change – *"Why do you look at the speck of sawdust in your brother's eye and pay no attention to the plank in your own eye?"* Luke 6:41, 42 NIV; *"Get thee out of thy country, and from thy kindred, and from thy father's house, unto a land that I will shew thee"* Genesis 12:1.

2. Into what trap can a "housewife" fall? *(circle one) (page 112)*

    a. having too many children

    b. soap opera addiction

    c. putting her house ahead of her husband

3. Into what trap can a mother fall? *(circle one) (page 113)*

    a. wedging herself between father and children

    b. too much driving

    c. busy-ness

4. In your opinion, what can husbands do in such situations?

    _____

    _____

5. What does a wife need to do in such situations? *(page 113)*

    _____

    _____

For Further Study

Men as godly leaders – *"Must manage his own family well and see that his children obey him with proper respect … must manage his children and his household well"* 1 Timothy 3:4, 12 NIV
Love – *"Doth not behave itself unseemly, seeketh not her own, is not easily provoked, thinketh no evil"*
1 Corinthians 13:5

E. Peace is brought into the home through: *(circle one) (page 113)*

   a. righteous living   b. screaming "be quiet"   c. staying away as much as possible

   1. When all is going according to our expectations, we can pray in victory. *(page 115)*

      ___ True ___ False

   2. When things do not fit our plans, we need to: *(circle all that apply) (page 115)*

      a. make adjustments   b. fall apart   c. go to our knees

Practical:

   1. Read Psalm 34:6.

   2. Write out Luke 10:5.

      _____

      _____

   Discuss with your spouse or friend: What part do you play in achieving peace in your home? What part have you played in breaking the peace in your home?

For Further Study

Peace at home – *"The Lord bless thee, and keep thee: The Lord make his face shine upon thee, and be gracious unto thee: The Lord lift up his countenance upon thee, and give thee peace"* Numbers 6:24-26; *"Seek peace, and pursue it"* Psalm 34:14; 1 Peter 3:11; *"A sound heart is the life of the flesh"* Proverbs 14:30; *"A soft answer turneth away wrath: but grievous words stir up anger"* Proverbs 15:1; *"Better is a dry morsel, and quietness therewith, than a house full of sacrifices with strife"* Proverbs 17:1; *"Let the peace of Christ rule in your hearts … you were called to peace"* Colossians 3:15 NIV; *"Now the Lord of peace himself give you peace always by all means"* 2 Thessalonians 3:16; *"Now the just shall live by faith … we are … of them that believe to the saving of the soul"* Hebrews 10:38, 39.

3.   Make some plans! If your spouse accepted you when you made a bad decision, what can you do TODAY to show your appreciation?

_____

Repeat this prayer out loud:

Father, my life is certainly less than perfect, and I am deeply grateful for the abundance of Your grace that covers all my sins and the sins of my household. I ask You to help me commit these lessons to my heart in revelation power so I will do more than simply make resolutions. I commit myself and my family to You. Amen.

Principles I want to memorize:

Self Test *Lesson 9*

1.   Men tend to make accusations, while women tend to give ultimatums.

    ___ True   ___ False

2.   What is one of the hardest things for a man to do?

    _____

3.   What is one of the hardest things for a woman to do?

    _____

4.   What precedes success?

    _____

5.   Men are stewards of _____.

6.   What is actually happening when a woman tries to change a man's nature?

    _____

7.   For whom is change often harder? *(circle one)*

    a. for a man who must trust God

    b. for a woman who must trust both God and her husband

8.   What results in peace?

    _____

Keep this test for your records.

Lesson 10
Wise Wives and Hardened Husbands

Lesson 10
Wise Wives and Hardened Husbands

A. What philosophy is the core of humanism? *(circle one) (page 119)*

self as God   tune in, turn on, drop out   Zoroastrianism

1. Where did this philosophy begin? *(circle one) (page 119)*

    a. Inca Empire   b. Timothy Leary   c. Garden of Eden

2. What is God's two-fold right of possession to man? *(page 119)*

    a. _____

    b. _____

3. What is sin basically? *(circle one) (page 119)*

    a. denial of God's right of possession

    b. doing bad things

    c. thinking bad thoughts

4. How did God unite man with Himself? *(circle one) (page 119)*

    a. by making him sinless

    b. by tempting him to sin

    c. by redeeming him from sin

For Further Study
Self as God – *"The way of a fool is right in his own eyes"* Proverbs 12:15; Proverbs 14:12; 16:2, 25.
Man is not God – *"Many are the plans in a man's heart, but it is the Lord's purpose that prevails"* Proverbs 19:21 NIV; Psalm 33:11; Proverbs 16:9; 20:24.

5.   Read John 10:10 and 1 John 3:8b.

B.   Write out 2 Corinthians 6:14.

_____

_____

1.   Is it an impossible situation when only one spouse is saved? *(circle all that apply) (page 120)*

   a. It is extremely difficult.

   b. Yes, one must leave.

   c. No, God is a miracle worker.

2.   It's not a good idea for the saved spouse to tell the other about Jesus. *(page 121)*

   ___ True   ___ False

3.   What can a man do to help his wife know Christ? *(page 121)*

   ___ Fast and pray   ___ Insist she attend church

C.   What is the greatest need in your life? *(page 122)*

_____

For Further Study

Satan's strategy – *"Your enemy the devil prowls around like a roaring lion looking for someone to devour"*
1 Peter 5:8 NIV.
God's purposes – *"I was delivered out of the mouth of the lion. And the Lord shall deliver me from every evil work, and will preserve me unto his heavenly kingdom: to whom be glory for ever and ever. Amen"*
2 Timothy 4:17, 18; *"For God so loved the world, that he gave his only begotten Son, that whosoever believeth in him should not perish, but have everlasting life"* John 3:16.

Define the following: *(page 122)*

1. Knowledge: _____

2. Understanding: _____

3. Wisdom: _____

D. What is the beginning of wisdom? *(page 122)*

1. Read James 3:15, Proverbs 3:7 and Proverbs 9:10.

2. What do you need to have dominion over the devil? *(circle all that apply) (page 122)*

    a. the fear of the Lord   b. a good pastor   c. the wisdom of God

3. Read James 1:5. What are we to do if we lack wisdom? *(page 122)*

    _____

4. Why does it make sense to trust God? *(circle all that apply) (page 123)*

    a. We don't know all.

    b. We can't see perfectly.

    c. We can't understand everything.

For Further Study

An unsaved spouse – *"The effectual fervent prayer of a righteous man availeth much"* James 5:16; *"The fear of the LORD is the beginning of wisdom: a good understanding have all they that do his commandments: his praise endureth for ever"* Psalm 111:10; Psalms 19:9-11; 129; 130.

5.   What do alcoholics, abusers, adulterers and addicts have in common? *(circle one)* *(page 123)*

    a. They attend the same church.

    b. They are liars.

    c. They know how to get away with it.

6.   All a man needs is the love of a good woman. *(page 123)*   ___ True   ___ False

E.   Exterior beauty cannot compare with _____. *(page 124)*

1.   Read 1 Peter 3:1-5.

2.   Name the barriers that need to be broken to talk to an unsaved spouse about Christ. *(page 125)*

    a. _____

    b. _____

    c. _____

For Further Study

If we lack wisdom – *"Behold, thou desirest truth in the inward parts: and in the hidden part thou shalt make me to know wisdom"* Psalm 51:6.

The benefits of wisdom – Proverbs 2:1-10

Ask God – Matthew 7:7-11 – *"And this is the confidence that we have in him, that, if we ask any thing according to his will, he heareth us: And if we know that he hear us, whatsoever we ask, we know that we have the petitions that we desired of him"* 1 John 5:14, 15.

3.   Circle three wrong things to do when listening to your spouse. *(page 125)*

a. nod in understanding

b. interrupt

c. challenge her

d. acknowledge occasionally with a "hmm"

e. correct her

f. look directly at her

F.   Solve the following problems by drawing a line to the matching remedy on the right. *(page 125)*

1. battered spouse   a. pray
2. war in the heart   b. leave
3. betrayed   c. stay away
4. persecuted   d. love

5.   To solve problems, you need wisdom for a strategy that leads to what? *(circle one) (page 125)*

a. Paradise   b. Divorce   c. VICTORY!

G.   Name some cultural differences that put strain on a marriage. *(page 126)*

_____

_____

For Further Study

Internal loveliness – *"Love endures long and is patient and kind; love never is envious nor boils over with jealousy, is not boastful or vainglorious, does not display itself haughtily. It is not conceited (arrogant and inflated with pride); it is not rude (unmannerly) and does not act unbecomingly. Love (God's love in us) does not insist on its own rights or its own way, for it is not self-seeking; it is not touchy or fretful or resentful; it takes no account of the evil done to it (it pays no attention to a suffered wrong)"* 1 Corinthians 13:4, 5 AMP.

Practical:

1. A "lion's den" was described as a place of irrational thoughts, emotions and motives, including jealousy, envy, anger, hate, malice, vengeance, greed, strife, spite and criticism. *(page 124)*
   In what way have you made your home a "lion's den"?

   _____

   _____

2. Bill married Jane because she was beautiful and fun. Now that they have children, he feels the responsibility of providing a Christian home. But Jane wasn't raised as a Christian and thinks Bill is over-protective. Based on what you've learned in this chapter, what advice would you give Bill?

   _____

   _____

3. Have cultural differences affected your marriage? In what way?

   _____

Repeat this prayer out loud:

Father, thank You for all the goodness my (future) marriage already holds and for giving me insight into how to do even better. Please start with me. Purify my heart and help me lead in righteousness. Amen.

For Further Study

Pray for the spouse's highest good – *"For I know the thoughts and plans that I have for you … thoughts and plans for welfare and peace and not for evil, to give you hope in your final outcome"* Jeremiah 29:11 AMP; Psalms 9:18; 37:1-11; Proverbs 23:18; 24:14.
Keep speech pure – *"By long forbearance and calmness of spirit a judge or ruler is persuaded, and soft speech breaks down the most bonelike resistance"* Proverbs 25:15 AMP.
The Word is our mirror – *"Thy word is a lamp unto my feet"* Psalm 119:104, 105.

Self Test *Lesson 10*

1. What is at the core of humanism? _____

2. What is the basis for God's "right of possession"? _____

3. What is sin basically? *(circle one)*

    a. denial of God's right of possession   b. doing bad things   c. thinking bad thoughts

4. What can a man do to help his wife know Christ?   ___ Fast and pray   ___ Insist she attend church

5. What is the difference between knowledge and wisdom?

    _____

    _____

6. What is the beginning of wisdom? _____

7. What do you need to have dominion over the devil? *(circle all that apply)*

    a. the fear of the Lord   b. a good pastor   c. the wisdom of God

8. What are we to do if we lack wisdom? _____

9. What do alcoholics, abusers, adulterers and addicts have in common?_____

10. All a man needs is the love of a good woman.   ___ True ___ False

11. Circle three wrong things to do when listening to your spouse.

    a. nod in understanding   c. challenge her   e. correct her

    b. interrupt   d. acknowledge occasionally with a "hmm"   f. look directly at her

12. To solve problems, you need wisdom for a strategy that leads to what? *(circle one)*

    a. Paradise   b. Divorce   c. VICTORY!

Keep this test for your records.

Lesson 11
Don't Die at Home

Lesson 11
Don't Die at Home

A. In what ways have devoted mothers been belittled by today's society? *(page 131)*

_____

_____

Write the main point of Isaiah 5:20.

_____

B. Fill in the blanks in the sentences with the words from the list below: *(page 132)*

future   seeds   family   parents   womb   society

1. Today's _____ is the _____ of tomorrow's _____.

2. Today's _____ are those who impregnate it with the _____ of the

_____.

C. Name some things wrong in today's world that are different from the last generation. *(page 132)*

_____

For Further Study

Today's parents impregnate tomorrow's society with the seeds of the future – Psalm 1:3; Jeremiah 17:7; *"When our sons shall be as plants grown large in their youth and our daughters as sculptured corner pillars hewn like those of a palace"* Psalm 144:12 AMP; *"Your wife shall be like a fruitful vine in the innermost parts of your house; your children shall be like olive plants round about your table"* Psalm 128:3 AMP.

1. Read 2 Timothy 2:13 and 3 John 4.

2. What was Apostle John's greatest joy? *(page 133)*

_____

D. What is an absolute vital element in parenting? *(circle one) (page 134)*

unity between parents   celebrity advice   Dr. Dobson's book

1. What happens when parents disagree in front of their children? *(circle one) (page 134)*

   a. They scare the children.
   b. They embarrass their friends.
   c. They lose authority.

2. The place of agreement is what? *(circle one) (page 134)*

   a. The biggest compromise
   b. The place of power
   c. The high ground

3. How can a child "take over" a home? *(page 134)*

_____

For Further Study

Unity between parents – "*And knowing their thoughts, He said to them, Any kingdom that is divided against itself is being brought to desolation and laid waste, and no city or house divided against itself will last or continue to stand*" Matthew 12:25 AMP; "*Behold, how good and how pleasant it is for brethren to dwell together in unity! It is like the precious ointment upon the head … As the dew of Hermon, and as the dew that descended upon the mountains of Zion: for there the LORD commanded the blessing, even life for evermore*" Psalm 133:1; "*Be eager and strive earnestly to guard and keep the harmony and oneness of [and produced by] the Spirit in the binding power of peace*" Ephesians 4:3 AMP.

Examples of unity – Disciples in the Upper Room – Acts 1:14; Peter's miraculous release from prison – Acts 12:5-11
Unity results from love – Colossians 3:14.

4.   What is one of the most important things for parents to agree on? *(circle one)* *(page 134)*

   a. television watching   b. children's nutrition   c. values

E.   List three things vital to normalcy in home life. *(page 134)*

   1. _____   2. _____   3. _____

F.   Discipline must be based on: *(page 134)*   ___ Correction   ___ Punishment

   1.   Punishing a son or daughter for doing wrong is in itself wrong unless: *(circle one)* *(page 134)*

      a. you've warned them three times

      b. you've first taught them how to do it right

      c. you chastise only verbally, not spank

   2.   What do mediocre men want? *(circle one)* *(page 134)*

      a. accountability   b. authority   c. action

   3.   Why do mediocre men abandon the position of disciplinarian and decision maker? *(page 134)*

      _____

      _____

For Further Study

Discipline is necessary – Proverbs 22:6, 15; Hebrews 12:10, 11; *"He will die for lack of discipline and instruction"* Proverbs 5:23; 23:13, 14 AMP.

Discipline must be done in love – Proverbs 13:24; Hebrews 12:5-7; *"Discipline your son while there is hope, but do not [indulge your angry resentments by undue chastisements and] set yourself to his ruin"* Proverbs 19:18 AMP.

A parent's greatest joy – *"My son, if your heart is wise, My own heart also will be glad; And my inmost being will rejoice When your lips speak what is right"* Proverbs 23:15, 16 NASB.

G. Mark "T" for True and "F" for False. *(pages 135-136)*

_____   1. Marriage is a hundred-hundred proposition.

_____   2. Being responsible for children is "women's work."

_____   3. One reason men don't know more about children is lack of information.

_____   4. Entertainment can be like a drug in that it is a form of escape.

_____   5. Men generally learn about relationships best intuitively.

H. Prayer produces _____. *(page 136)*

1. Intercession is a form of _____. *(fill in the blank) (page 137)*

   a. dying to self   b. hiding from reality   c. ministry   d. intimacy

I. Name some forms of ministry. *(page 137)*

_____

_____

_____

For Further Study

Father's responsibilities for children – *"Fathers, do not irritate and provoke your children to anger [do not exasperate them to resentment], but rear them [tenderly] in the training and discipline and the counsel and admonition of the Lord"* Ephesians 6:4 AMP; *"Fathers, do not provoke or irritate or fret your children [do not be hard on them or harass them], lest they become discouraged and sullen and morose and feel inferior and frustrated [Do not break their spirit.]"* Colossians 3:21 AMP; 1 Timothy 3:4, 12.
Abraham's example – *"He will direct his children and his household after him to keep the way of the Lord by doing what is right and just"* Genesis 18:19 NIV.
Other examples – Job 29:11-25; Proverbs 31:10-31

1. What should take place at the dinner table. *(circle all that apply)* *(page 137)*

    a. "limit setting"

    b. communication

    c. minimal stress

    d. opportunity for ministry

2. Whose responsibility is taking a wife for granted? *(circle one)* *(page 137)*

    a. his   b. hers   c. both

3. Family calendar meetings help overcome the principle that "What people don't understand they are

    against." *(page 139)*   ___ True ___ False

J. Great parents rarely make mistakes. *(page 141)*   ___ True ___ False

    What determines the result of your failures? *(page 141)*

    _____

For Further Study

Bedtime, meals, housework and trips are opportunities for family ministry – Deuteronomy 6:6-9; 11:19; Proverbs 6:20-23.

Be a good home manager – 1 Timothy 5:14; Titus 2:4-5.

A mother's great reward – *"Her children rise up and call her blessed (happy, fortunate, and to be envied); and her husband boasts of and praises her"* Proverbs 31:28 AMP.

Practical:

1. In what ways can you encourage your (future) wife to look her best and to minister to you and the children?

   _____

2. Whose responsibility is it to raise your children?

   _____

3. What is the most important thing on your calendar? What does this say to your wife and children?

   _____

4. What does your (future) wife think about her 24-hour-a-day role of "mother"? Have you asked her? Does she need a break?

   _____

Repeat this prayer out loud:

Father, thank You for covering all my mistakes as a father and for protecting my family even from me. I surrender myself to You humbly today and ask You to make me a father after Your own pattern, starting with being a good husband to my wife. Thank You for hearing and answering my prayer. Amen.

Principles I want to memorize:

Self Test *Lesson 11*

1. Today's family is the _____ of tomorrow's society.

2. What was Apostle John's greatest joy? _____

3. An absolutely vital element in parenting is: *(circle one)*
    a. Learning to enjoy the same television programs
    b. Learning to discipline sons differently than daughters
    c. Learning not to disagree in front of your children

4. What three things are vital to having a normal home life?
    a. _____ b. _____ c. _____

5. Punishing sons and daughters for doing something wrong, when the parent has not first taught them how

    to do it right is _____.

6. Discipline must be based on: ___ Correction ___ Punishment

7. What do mediocre men want? *(circle one)*

    a. accountability   b. authority   c. action

8. Being responsible for children is "women's work."   ___ True   ___ False

9. Name some forms of ministry.

    _____

10. Family calendar meetings help overcome the principle that "What people don't understand they are against."

    ___ True   ___ False

11. Great parents rarely make mistakes.   ___ True   ___ False

Keep this test for your records.

Lesson 12
The Mature Woman

Lesson 12
The Mature Woman

A. Read: *"There is a time for everything, and a season for every activity under heaven: a time to be born and a time to die, a time to plant and a time to uproot"* Ecclesiastes 3:1-2 NIV.

1. Each season has a _____ of its own. *(fill in the blank) (page 147)*

    a. glory   b. problem   c. lesson

2. What is the determining factor as to whether the "season" is a blessing or a curse? *(page 147)*

    _____

3. Why is death an abnormality? *(page 148)*

    _____

B. Read 1 Timothy 5:3 and James 1:27.

1. In these verses, how does the Bible say we are to treat widows?

    _____

For Further Study
God takes us through seasons – Psalm 22:9-11; *"Listen to me, all you who are left in Israel. I created you and have cared for you since before you were born. I will be your God throughout your lifetime—until your hair is white with age. I made you, and I will care for you. I will carry you along and save you"* Isaiah 46:3, 4 NLT.

2. What responsibility does the Bible specifically give to the "aged" women? *(circle one)* *(page 148)*

    a. teaching the younger women

    b. raising money for the church kitchen

    c. encouraging each other in their "seniors" Sunday School class

3. Young people must learn from their mistakes, not the experience of others. *(pages 148-149)*

    ___ True   ___ False

C. Read: *"The glory of the young is their strength; the gray hair of experience is the splendor of the old"* Proverbs 20:29 NLT.

1. There is a _____ to every age of life. *(fill in the blank)* *(page 149)*

    a. glory   b. problem   c. lesson

2. Why do people often die soon after retirement? *(page 149)*

    _____

3. What is the "sin of being fifty"? *(page 150)*

    _____

    _____

For Further Study

Mature women's responsibility – *"Now that I am old and gray, do not abandon me, O God. Let me proclaim your power to this new generation, your mighty miracles to all who come after me"* Psalm 71:18 NLT; Psalms 78:4; 145:4; Joel 1:3.

Pursue productivity – *"Where there is no vision [no redemptive revelation of God], the people perish; but he who keeps the law [of God, which includes that of man]—blessed (happy, fortunate, and enviable) is he"* Proverbs 29:18 AMP.

4.   What would you summarize as a goal for old age? *(circle one) (page 150)*

a. don't quit   b. sleep a lot   c. take proper medicines

D.   Which Bible passage reads like a list of things to watch for as we mature? *(page 150)*

_____

1.   List some of the symptoms women deal with during menopause. *(pages 151-152)*

_____

2.   Is there good quality of life for a woman after the "change of life"? *(page 152)*

___ Yes ___ No

3.   In the older season of life, where do problems with children often occur? *(page 153)*

_____

4.   What do you do with bitterness over lost opportunities and regrets? *(circle one) (page 153)*

a. resolve it in prayer   b. forget about it   c. let it go

E.   Read 2 Peter 1:8, 15.

For Further Study

Grow and be strengthened in God – Ephesians 3:16-21; Philippians 4:13; Colossians 1:9-12; 1 Timothy 1:12; *"But the Lord stood at my side and gave me strength"* 2 Timothy 4:17 NIV; *"And now, all glory to God, who is able to keep you from stumbling, and who will bring you into his glorious presence innocent of sin and with great joy"* Jude 24 NLT.

Name some practical ways in which older people can serve others. *(page 154)*

_____

_____

_____

Practical:

1.   Whom would you regard as a "widow"? In what ways could you serve them?

_____

_____

2.   Think it over:

What are you investing in?
Are you going to end up friendless?
Will you face poverty in old age at the rate you are going?
Could you become estranged from your children?

Repeat this prayer out loud:

Father, in Jesus' Name, grant me the grace to grow old with Your wisdom, to learn how to communicate Your wonder and knowledge. Help me to be seen as an example of Your peace and goodness to my spouse, my children and my world. Thank You so much for investing so much into me. I will be a worthy investment of Your love, oh Lord. Thank You again, Amen.

Principles I want to memorize:

Self Test *Lesson 12*

1. Each season has a _____ of its own. *(fill in the blank)*

    a. glory   b. problem   c. lesson

2. Why is death an abnormality?

    _____

3. What responsibility does the Bible specifically give to the "aged" women? *(circle one)*

    a. teaching the younger women
    b. raising money for the church kitchen
    c. encouraging each other in their "seniors" Sunday School class

4. When women go through their "change of life," it signals the end of pleasure in their lives.

    ___ True ___ False

5. Why do people often die soon after retirement?

    _____

6. What is the "sin of being fifty"?

    _____

    _____

7. What are some things people can do to insure a good old age?

    a. _____

    b. _____

    c. _____

Keep this test for your records.

Final Exam   THE UNIQUE WOMAN

1. A life without value is _____. *(fill in the blank)*

   a. worthless   b. livable   c. happier

2. How is a woman's uniqueness basically satisfied?

   _____

3. On what are disappointments normally based? _____

4. What are the five reasons an entire generation wasn't able to enter Canaan?

   a. _____   d. _____

   b. _____   e. _____

   c. _____

5. Where are these sins listed in Scripture? *(give book and chapter)* _____

6. Women are not subject to the same temptations to sin as men.   ___ True   ___ False

7. Name the three basic temptations.

   a. _____

   b. _____

   c. _____

8. Scripture says no one who abides in Christ can habitually _____.

9. What sin would we be guilty of if we were demanding that God do something that was contrary

   to His Word? _____

10. Pornography is a form of: *(circle one)*

    a. murmuring   b. fornication   c. idolatry

11. When it comes to Christianity, _____ is the basic issue.

12. Who is responsible for a woman's intelligence, talents, abilities and gifts given to her by God? _____

13. Name some examples of courageous women in the Bible.

    _____   _____   _____   _____

14. What happens when women try to compete with men by copying them?

    _____

    _____

15. Women can be great achievers.   ___ True ___ False

16. Gifts and anointings are no substitute for: *(circle one)*

    a. marriage   b. ministry   c. obedience

17. What term do we use to describe God's ability to take things meant for evil and convert them to work

    for our good? _____

18. What can cause a man to "not get ready answers" to his prayers?

    _____

19. Give the Scriptural reference for this truth. *(give book, chapter and verse)* _____

20. The Bible teaches male dictatorship.   ___ True ___ False

21. Women who are being sexually or physically abused must continue to submit entirely to their husbands.

    ___ True ___ False

22. What image is often confused with our image of God? _____

23. Can forgiveness be the key to break the cycle of sins passed from one generation to another? ___ Yes ___ No

24. Christianity is built upon: *(circle one)*

    a. suppression   b. confession   c. repression

25. In what passage of Scripture can you find the principle of "release"? *(give book, chapter and verses)*

    _____

26. How is it possible to retain the sins of others? _____

27. Forgiving others is optional.   ___ True ___ False

28. It is blasphemous to think a person could need to "forgive" God.   ___ True ___ False

29. Forgiveness is never earned but is always a free gift.   ___ True ___ False

30. The Bible speaks of anything sexual as intrinsically evil.   ___ True ___ False

31. Sex is to be based on the desire to give, not to get.   ___ True ___ False

32. Sex is an external evidence of what? _____

33. Woman was created to be man's: *(circle one)*

    a. completer   b. competitor   c. predator

34. What does lust do?   ___ Limits ___ Releases

35. Name at least two areas of life that illustrate the principle that "All true joy is born out of sorrow."

    a. _____

    b. _____

36. Why does a single woman of good Christian character particularly need to be careful?

    _____

    _____

37. New construction is always harder than reconstruction. ___ True ___ False

38. God is a: ___ magician ___ miracle worker

39. Facing reality is: *(circle one)*
    a. the worst way to live   b. a boring way to live   c. the only way to live

40. We have a tendency to judge others by their _____ but ourselves by our _____.

41. A woman tends to dream of a man in terms of the: *(circle one)*
    a. unreal   b. ideal   c. free meal

42. Maturation is a lifelong process. ___ True ___ False

43. Selfishness is a trait of immaturity. ___ True ___ False

44. Crisis is normal to life. ___ True ___ False

45. If God truly joins two people together in marriage, they will have little or no problems.

    ___ True ___ False

46. What is one of the hardest things for a man to do? _____

47. What is one of the hardest things for a woman to do? _____

48. For whom is change often harder? *(circle one)*
    a. for a man who must trust God
    b. for a woman who must trust both God and her husband

49. What is sin basically? *(circle one)*
    a. denial of God's right of possession   b. doing bad things   c. thinking bad thoughts

50. What can a man do to help his wife know Christ? ___ Fast and pray ___ Insist she attend church

51. What is the beginning of wisdom? _____

52. What are we to do if we lack wisdom? _____

53. What do alcoholics, abusers, adulterers and addicts have in common? _____

54. All a man needs is the love of a good woman.   ___ True ___ False

55. What was Apostle John's greatest joy? _____

56. An absolutely vital element in parenting is: *(circle one)*
    a. learning to enjoy the same television programs
    b. learning to discipline sons differently than daughters
    c. learning not to disagree in front of your children

57. Punishing sons and daughters for doing something wrong when the parent has not first taught them how

    to do it right is _____.

58. Discipline must be based on: ___ Correction ___ Punishment

59. What do mediocre men want? *(circle one)*

    a. accountability   b. authority   c. action

60. Being responsible for children is "women's work."   ___ True ___ False

61. Great parents rarely make mistakes.   ___ True ___ False

62. Each season has a _____ of its own. *(fill in the blank)*

    a. glory   b. problem   c. lesson

63. What responsibility does the Bible specifically give to the "aged" women? *(circle one)*
    a. teaching the younger women
    b. raising money for the church kitchen
    c. encouraging each other in their "seniors" Sunday School class

DETACH HERE

64. Short essay: The Bible says, *"He called their name Adam"* Genesis 5:2. Adam and Eve both separately and jointly portray on earth the image of God. Explain how this can be, using personal illustrations and examples from the book.

_____

_____

_____

_____

_____

_____

_____

_____

_____

_____

_____

Name _____

Address _____ City _____ State ____ Zip _____

Telephone a.m. _____ p.m. _____

Email Address _____

The Final Exam is required to be "commissioned."

For more information, contact
Christian Men's Network | P.O. Box 93478 | Southlake, TX 76092
ChristianMensNetwork.com | office@ChristianMensNetwork.com | 817-437-4888

DETACH HERE

Basic Daily Bible Reading

Read Proverbs each morning for wisdom, Psalms each evening for courage. Make copies of this chart and keep it in your Bible to mark off as you read. If you are just starting the habit of Bible reading, be aware that longer translations or paraphrases (such as Amplified and Living) will take longer to read each day. As you start, it is okay to read only one of the chapters in Psalms each night, instead of the many listed. Mark your chart so you'll remember which ones you haven't read.
NOTE: The chronological chart following has the rest of the chapters of Psalms that are not listed here. By using both charts together, you will cover the entire book of Psalms.

Day of Month	Proverbs	Psalms	Day of Month	Proverbs	Psalms
1	1	1, 2, 4, 5, 6			
2	2	7, 8, 9	18	18	82, 83, 84, 85
3	3	10, 11, 12, 13, 14, 15	19	19	87, 88, 91, 92
4	4	16, 17, 19, 20	20	20	93, 94, 95, 97
5	5	21, 22, 23	21	21	98, 99, 100, 101, 103
6	6	24, 25, 26, 27	22	22	104, 108
7	7	28, 29, 31, 32	23	23	109, 110, 111
8	8	33, 35	24	24	112, 113, 114, 115, 117
9	9	36, 37	25	25	119:1-56
10	10	38, 39, 40	26	26	119:57-112
11	11	41, 42, 43, 45, 46	27	27	119:113-176
12	12	47, 48, 49, 50	28	28	120, 121, 122, 124, 130,
13	13	53, 55, 58, 61, 62			131, 133, 134
14	14	64, 65, 66, 67	29	29	135, 136, 138
15	15	68, 69	30	30	139, 140, 141, 143
16	16	70, 71, 73	31	31	144, 145, 146, 148, 150
17	17	75, 76, 77, 81			

Chronological Annual Bible Reading

This schedule follows the events of the Bible chronologically and can be used with any translation or paraphrase of the Bible. Each day has an average of 77 verses of Scripture. If you follow this annually, along with your Daily Bible Reading, by your third year, you will recognize where you are and what is going to happen next. By your fifth year, you will understand the Scriptural background and setting for any reference spoken of in a message or book. At that point, the Word will become more like "meat" to you and less like "milk." Once you understand the basic stories and what happens on the surface, God can reveal to you the layers of meaning beneath. So, make copies of this chart to keep in your Bible and mark off as you read. And start reading—it's the greatest adventure in life!

Some notes:
1. Some modern translations don't have verses numbered (such as The Message), so they cannot be used with this chart. Also, if you are just starting the Bible, be aware that longer translations or paraphrases (such as Amplified and Living) tend to take longer to read each day.
2. The Daily Bible Reading chart covers the Proverbs and the chapters of Psalms that are not listed here. By using both charts together, you will cover the entire books of Psalms and Proverbs along with the rest of the Bible.
3. The chronology of Scripture is obvious in some cases, educated guesswork in others. The placement of Job, for example, is purely conjecture since there is no consensus among Bible scholars as to its date or place. For the most part, however, chronological reading helps the reader, since it places stories that have duplicated information, or prophetic utterances elsewhere in Scripture, within the same reading sequence.

HOW TO READ SCRIPTURE NOTATIONS:
Book chapter: verse. (Mark 15:44 means the book of Mark, chapter 15, verse 44.)
Book chapter; chapter (Mark 15; 16; 17 means the book of Mark, chapters 15, 16, 17.)
Books continue the same until otherwise noted. (2 Kings 22; 23:1-28; Jeremiah 20 means the book of 2 Kings, chapter 22, the book of 2 Kings, chapter 23, verses 1-28; then the book of Jeremiah, chapter 20.)

MAJORING IN MEN®

1	Jan 1	Genesis 1; 2; 3
2	Jan 2	Genesis 4; 5; 6
3	Jan 3	Genesis 7; 8; 9
4	Jan 4	Genesis 10; 11; 12
5	Jan 5	Genesis 13; 14; 15; 16
6	Jan 6	Genesis 17; 18; 19:1-29
7	Jan 7	Genesis 19:30-38; 20; 21
8	Jan 8	Genesis 22; 23; 24:1-31
9	Jan 9	Genesis 24:32-67; 25
10	Jan 10	Genesis 26; 27
11	Jan 11	Genesis 28; 29; 30:1-24
12	Jan 12	Genesis 30:25-43; 31
13	Jan 13	Genesis 32; 33; 34
14	Jan 14	Genesis 35; 36
15	Jan 15	Genesis 37; 38; 39
16	Jan 16	Genesis 40; 41
17	Jan 17	Genesis 42; 43
18	Jan 18	Genesis 44; 45
19	Jan 19	Genesis 46; 47; 48
20	Jan 20	Genesis 49; 50; Exodus 1
21	Jan 21	Exodus 2; 3; 4
22	Jan 22	Exodus 5; 6; 7
23	Jan 23	Exodus 8; 9
24	Jan 24	Exodus 10; 11; 12
25	Jan 25	Exodus 13; 14; 15
26	Jan 26	Exodus 16; 17; 18
27	Jan 27	Exodus 19; 20; 21
28	Jan 28	Exodus 22; 23; 24
29	Jan 29	Exodus 25; 26
30	Jan 30	Exodus 27; 28; 29:1-28
31	Jan 31	Exodus 29:29-46; 30; 31
32	Feb 1	Exodus 32; 33; 34
33	Feb 2	Exodus 35; 36
34	Feb 3	Exodus 37; 38
35	Feb 4	Exodus 39; 40
36	Feb 5	Leviticus 1; 2; 3; 4
37	Feb 6	Leviticus 5; 6; 7
38	Feb 7	Leviticus 8; 9; 10
39	Feb 8	Leviticus 11; 12; 13:1-37
40	Feb 9	Leviticus 13:38-59; 14
41	Feb 10	Leviticus 15; 16
42	Feb 11	Leviticus 17; 18; 19
43	Feb 12	Leviticus 20; 21; 22:1-16
44	Feb 13	Leviticus 22:17-33; 23
45	Feb 14	Leviticus 24; 25
46	Feb 15	Leviticus 26; 27
47	Feb 16	Numbers 1; 2
48	Feb 17	Numbers 3; 4:1-20
49	Feb 18	Numbers 4:21-49; 5; 6
50	Feb 19	Numbers 7
51	Feb 20	Numbers 8; 9; 10
52	Feb 21	Numbers 11; 12; 13
53	Feb 22	Numbers 14; 15
54	Feb 23	Numbers 16; 17
55	Feb 24	Numbers 18; 19; 20
56	Feb 25	Numbers 21; 22
57	Feb 26	Numbers 23; 24; 25
58	Feb 27	Numbers 26; 27
59	Feb 28	Numbers 28; 29; 30
60	Mar 1	Numbers 31; 32:1-27
61	Mar 2	Numbers 32:28-42; 33
62	Mar 3	Numbers 34; 35; 36
63	Mar 4	Deuteronomy 1; 2
64	Mar 5	Deuteronomy 3; 4
65	Mar 6	Deuteronomy 5; 6; 7
66	Mar 7	Deuteronomy 8; 9; 10
67	Mar 8	Deuteronomy 11; 12; 13
68	Mar 9	Deuteronomy 14; 15; 16
69	Mar 10	Deuteronomy 17; 18; 19; 20
70	Mar 11	Deuteronomy 21; 22; 23
71	Mar 12	Deuteronomy 24; 25; 26; 27
72	Mar 13	Deuteronomy 28
73	Mar 14	Deuteronomy 29; 30; 31
74	Mar 15	Deuteronomy 32; 33
75	Mar 16	Deuteronomy 34; Psalm 90; Joshua 1; 2
76	Mar 17	Joshua 3; 4; 5; 6
77	Mar 18	Joshua 7; 8; 9
78	Mar 19	Joshua 10; 11
79	Mar 20	Joshua 12; 13; 14
80	Mar 21	Joshua 15; 16
81	Mar 22	Joshua 17; 18; 19:1-23
82	Mar 23	Joshua 19:24-51; 20; 21
83	Mar 24	Joshua 22; 23; 24
84	Mar 25	Judges 1; 2; 3:1-11
85	Mar 26	Judges 3:12-31; 4; 5
86	Mar 27	Judges 6; 7
87	Mar 28	Judges 8; 9
88	Mar 29	Judges 10; 11; 12
89	Mar 30	Judges 13; 14; 15
90	Mar 31	Judges 16; 17; 18
91	Apr 1	Judges 19; 20

[You have completed 1/4 of the Bible!]

92	Apr 2	Judges 21; Job 1; 2; 3
93	Apr 3	Job 4; 5; 6
94	Apr 4	Job 7; 8; 9
95	Apr 5	Job 10; 11; 12
96	Apr 6	Job 13; 14; 15
97	Apr 7	Job 16; 17; 18; 19
98	Apr 8	Job 20; 21
99	Apr 9	Job 22; 23; 24
100	Apr 10	Job 25; 26; 27; 28
101	Apr 11	Job 29; 30; 31
102	Apr 12	Job 32; 33; 34
103	Apr 13	Job 35; 36; 37
104	Apr 14	Job 38; 39
105	Apr 15	Job 40; 41; 42
106	Apr 16	Ruth 1; 2; 3
107	Apr 17	Ruth 4; 1 Samuel 1; 2
108	Apr 18	1 Samuel 3; 4; 5; 6
109	Apr 19	1 Samuel 7; 8; 9
110	Apr 20	1 Samuel 10; 11; 12; 13
111	Apr 21	1 Samuel 14; 15
112	Apr 22	1 Samuel 16; 17
113	Apr 23	1 Samuel 18; 19; Psalm 59
114	Apr 24	1 Samuel 20; 21; Psalms 34; 56
115	Apr 25	1 Samuel 22; 23, Psalms 52; 142
116	Apr 26	1 Samuel 24; 25; 1 Chronicles 12:8-18; Psalm 57
117	Apr 27	1 Samuel 26; 27; 28; Psalms 54; 63
118	Apr 28	1 Samuel 29; 30; 31; 1 Chronicles 12:1-7; 12:19-22
119	Apr 29	1 Chronicles 10; 2 Samuel 1; 2
120	Apr 30	2 Samuel 3; 4; 1 Chronicles 11:1-9; 12:23-40
121	May 1	2 Samuel 5; 6; 1 Chronicles 13; 14
122	May 2	2 Samuel 22; 1 Chronicles 15
123	May 3	1 Chronicles 16; Psalm 18
124	May 4	2 Samuel 7; Psalms 96; 105
125	May 5	1 Chronicles 17; 2 Samuel 8; 9; 10
126	May 6	1 Chronicles 18; 19; Psalm 60; 2 Samuel 11
127	May 7	2 Samuel 12; 13; 1 Chronicles 20:1-3; Psalm 51
128	May 8	2 Samuel 14; 15
129	May 9	2 Samuel 16; 17; 18; Psalm 3
130	May 10	2 Samuel 19; 20; 21
131	May 11	2 Samuel 23:8-23
132	May 12	1 Chronicles 20:4-8; 11:10-25; 2 Samuel 23:24-39; 24
133	May 13	1 Chronicles 11:26-47; 21; 22
134	May 14	1 Chronicles 23; 24; Psalm 30
135	May 15	1 Chronicles 25; 26
136	May 16	1 Chronicles 27; 28; 29
137	May 17	1 Kings 1; 2:1-12; 2 Samuel 23:1-7
138	May 18	1 Kings 2:13-46; 3; 2 Chronicles 1:1-13
139	May 19	1 Kings 5; 6; 2 Chronicles 2
140	May 20	1 Kings 7; 2 Chronicles 3; 4
141	May 21	1 Kings 8; 2 Chronicles 5
142	May 22	1 Kings 9; 2 Chronicles 6; 7:1-10
143	May 23	1 Kings 10:1-13; 2 Chronicles 7:11-22; 8; 9:1-12; 1 Kings 4
144	May 24	1 Kings 10:14-29; 2 Chronicles 1:14-17; 9:13-28; Psalms 72; 127
145	May 25	Song of Solomon 1; 2; 3; 4; 5
146	May 26	Song of Solomon 6; 7; 8; 1 Kings 11:1-40
147	May 27	Ecclesiastes 1; 2; 3; 4
148	May 28	Ecclesiastes 5; 6; 7; 8
149	May 29	Ecclesiastes 9; 10; 11; 12; 1 Kings 11:41-43; 2 Chronicles 9:29-31
150	May 30	1 Kings 12; 2 Chronicles 10; 11
151	May 31	1 Kings 13; 14; 2 Chronicles 12
152	June 1	1 Kings 15; 2 Chronicles 13; 14; 15
153	June 2	1 Kings 16; 2 Chronicles 16; 17
154	June 3	1 Kings 17; 18; 19
155	June 4	1 Kings 20; 21
156	June 5	1 Kings 22; 2 Chronicles 18
157	June 6	2 Kings 1; 2; 2 Chronicles 19; 20; 21:1-3
158	June 7	2 Kings 3; 4
159	June 8	2 Kings 5; 6; 7
160	June 9	2 Kings 8; 9; 2 Chronicles 21:4-20
161	June 10	2 Chronicles 22; 23; 2 Kings 10; 11
162	June 11	Joel 1; 2; 3
163	June 12	2 Kings 12; 13; 2 Chronicles 24
164	June 13	2 Kings 14; 2 Chronicles 25; Jonah 1
165	June 14	Jonah 2; 3; 4; Hosea 1; 2; 3; 4
166	June 15	Hosea 5; 6; 7; 8; 9; 10
167	June 16	Hosea 11; 12; 13; 14

168	June 17	2 Kings 15:1-7; 2 Chronicles 26; Amos 1; 2; 3
169	June 18	Amos 4; 5; 6; 7
170	June 19	Amos 8; 9; 2 Kings 15:8-18; Isaiah 1
171	June 20	Isaiah 2; 3; 4; 2 Kings 15:19-38; 2 Chronicles 27
172	June 21	Isaiah 5; 6; Micah 1; 2; 3
173	June 22	Micah 4; 5; 6; 7; 2 Kings 16:1-18
174	June 23	2 Chronicles 28; Isaiah 7; 8
175	June 24	Isaiah 9; 10; 11; 12
176	June 25	Isaiah 13; 14; 15; 16
177	June 26	Isaiah 17; 18; 19; 20; 21
178	June 27	Isaiah 22; 23; 24; 25
179	June 28	Isaiah 26; 27; 28; 29
180	June 29	Isaiah 30; 31; 32; 33
181	June 30	Isaiah 34; 35; 2 Kings 18:1-8; 2 Chronicles 29
182	July 1	2 Chronicles 30; 31; 2 Kings 17; 2 Kings 16:19-20
		[You have completed 1/2 of the Bible!]
183	July 2	2 Kings 18:9-37; 2 Chronicles 32:1-19; Isaiah 36
184	July 3	2 Kings 19; 2 Chronicles 32:20-23; Isaiah 37
185	July 4	2 Kings 20; 21:1-18; 2 Chronicles 32:24-33; Isaiah 38; 39
186	July 5	2 Chronicles 33:1-20; Isaiah 40; 41
187	July 6	Isaiah 42; 43; 44
188	July 7	Isaiah 45; 46; 47; 48
189	July 8	Isaiah 49; 50; 51; 52
190	July 9	Isaiah 53; 54; 55; 56; 57
191	July 10	Isaiah 58; 59; 60; 61; 62
192	July 11	Isaiah 63; 64; 65; 66
193	July 12	2 Kings 21:19-26; 2 Chronicles 33:21-25; 34:1-7; Zephaniah 1; 2; 3
194	July 13	Jeremiah 1; 2; 3
195	July 14	Jeremiah 4; 5
196	July 15	Jeremiah 6; 7; 8
197	July 16	Jeremiah 9; 10; 11
198	July 17	Jeremiah 12; 13; 14; 15
199	July 18	Jeremiah 16; 17; 18; 19
200	July 19	Jeremiah 20; 2 Kings 22; 23:1-28
201	July 20	2 Chronicles 34:8-33; 35:1-19; Nahum 1; 2; 3
202	July 21	2 Kings 23:29-37; 2 Chronicles 35:20-27; 36:1-5; Jeremiah 22:10-17; 26; Habakkuk 1
203	July 22	Habakkuk 2; 3; Jeremiah 46; 47; 2 Kings 24:1-4; 2 Chronicles 36:6-7
204	July 23	Jeremiah 25; 35; 36; 45
205	July 24	Jeremiah 48; 49:1-33
206	July 25	Daniel 1; 2
207	July 26	Jeremiah 22:18-30; 2 Kings 24:5-20; 2 Chronicles 36:8-12; Jeremiah 37:1-2; 52:1-3; 24; 29
208	July 27	Jeremiah 27; 28; 23
209	July 28	Jeremiah 50; 51:1-19
210	July 29	Jeremiah 51:20-64; 49:34-39; 34
211	July 30	Ezekiel 1; 2; 3; 4
212	July 31	Ezekiel 5; 6; 7; 8

213	Aug 1	Ezekiel 9; 10; 11; 12
214	Aug 2	Ezekiel 13, 14, 15, 16:1-34
215	Aug 3	Ezekiel 16:35-63; 17; 18
216	Aug 4	Ezekiel 19; 20
217	Aug 5	Ezekiel 21; 22
218	Aug 6	Ezekiel 23; 2 Kings 25:1; 2 Chronicles 36:13-16; Jeremiah 39:1; 52:4; Ezekiel 24
219	Aug 7	Jeremiah 21; 22:1-9; 32; 30
220	Aug 8	Jeremiah 31; 33; Ezekiel 25
221	Aug 9	Ezekiel 29:1-16; 30; 31; 26
222	Aug 10	Ezekiel 27; 28; Jeremiah 37:3-21
223	Aug 11	Jeremiah 38; 39:2-10; 52:5-30
224	Aug 12	2 Kings 25:2-22; 2 Chronicles 36:17-21; Jeremiah 39:11-18; 40:1-6; Lamentations 1
225	Aug 13	Lamentations 2; 3
226	Aug 14	Lamentations 4; 5; Obadiah; Jeremiah 40:7-16
227	Aug 15	Jeremiah 41; 42; 43; 44; 2 Kings 25:23-26
228	Aug 16	Ezekiel 33:21-33; 34; 35; 36
229	Aug 17	Ezekiel 37; 38; 39
230	Aug 18	Ezekiel 32; 33:1-20; Daniel 3
231	Aug 19	Ezekiel 40; 41
232	Aug 20	Ezekiel 42; 43; 44
233	Aug 21	Ezekiel 45; 46; 47
234	Aug 22	Ezekiel 48; 29:17-21; Daniel 4
235	Aug 23	Jeremiah 52:31-34; 2 Kings 25:27-30; Psalms 44; 74; 79
236	Aug 24	Psalms 80; 86; 89
237	Aug 25	Psalms 102; 106
238	Aug 26	Psalms 123; 137; Daniel 7; 8
239	Aug 27	Daniel 5; 9; 6
240	Aug 28	2 Chronicles 36:22-23; Ezra 1; 2
241	Aug 29	Ezra 3; 4:1-5; Daniel 10; 11
242	Aug 30	Daniel 12; Ezra 4:6-24; 5; 6:1-13; Haggai 1
243	Aug 31	Haggai 2; Zechariah 1; 2; 3
244	Sept 1	Zechariah 4; 5; 6; 7; 8
245	Sept 2	Ezra 6:14-22; Psalm 78
246	Sept 3	Psalms 107; 116; 118
247	Sept 4	Psalms 125; 126; 128; 129; 132; 147
248	Sept 5	Psalm 149; Zechariah 9; 10; 11; 12; 13
249	Sept 6	Zechariah 14; Esther 1; 2; 3
250	Sept 7	Esther 4; 5; 6; 7; 8
251	Sept 8	Esther 9; 10; Ezra 7; 8
252	Sept 9	Ezra 9; 10; Nehemiah 1
253	Sept 10	Nehemiah 2; 3; 4; 5
254	Sept 11	Nehemiah 6; 7
255	Sept 12	Nehemiah 8; 9; 10
256	Sept 13	Nehemiah 11; 12
257	Sept 14	Nehemiah 13; Malachi 1; 2; 3; 4
258	Sept 15	1 Chronicles 1; 2:1-35
259	Sept 16	1 Chronicles 2:36-55; 3; 4
260	Sept 17	1 Chronicles 5; 6:1-41
261	Sept 18	1 Chronicles 6:42-81; 7
262	Sept 19	1 Chronicles 8; 9
263	Sept 20	Matthew 1; 2; 3; 4

264	Sept 21	Matthew 5; 6
265	Sept 22	Matthew 7; 8
266	Sept 23	Matthew 9; 10
267	Sept 24	Matthew 11; 12
268	Sept 25	Matthew 13; 14
269	Sept 26	Matthew 15; 16
270	Sept 27	Matthew 17; 18; 19
271	Sept 28	Matthew 20; 21
272	Sept 29	Matthew 22; 23
273	Sept 30	Matthew 24; 25
		[You have completed 3/4 of the Bible!]
274	Oct 1	Matthew 26; 27; 28
275	Oct 2	Mark 1; 2
276	Oct 3	Mark 3; 4
277	Oct 4	Mark 5; 6
278	Oct 5	Mark 7; 8:1-26
279	Oct 6	Mark 8:27-38; 9
280	Oct 7	Mark 10; 11
281	Oct 8	Mark 12; 13
282	Oct 9	Mark 14
283	Oct 10	Mark 15; 16
284	Oct 11	Luke 1
285	Oct 12	Luke 2; 3
286	Oct 13	Luke 4; 5
287	Oct 14	Luke 6; 7:1-23
288	Oct 15	Luke 7:24-50; 8
289	Oct 16	Luke 9
290	Oct 17	Luke 10; 11
291	Oct 18	Luke 12; 13
292	Oct 19	Luke 14; 15
293	Oct 20	Luke 16; 17
294	Oct 21	Luke 18; 19
295	Oct 22	Luke 20; 21
296	Oct 23	Luke 22
297	Oct 24	Luke 23; 24:1-28
298	Oct 25	Luke 24:29-53; John 1
299	Oct 26	John 2; 3; 4:1-23
300	Oct 27	John 4:24-54; 5; 6:1-7
301	Oct 28	John 6:8-71; 7:1-21
302	Oct 29	John 7:22-53; 8
303	Oct 30	John 9; 10
304	Oct 31	John 11; 12:1-28
305	Nov 1	John 12:29-50; 13; 14
306	Nov 2	John 15; 16; 17
307	Nov 3	John 18; 19:1-24
308	Nov 4	John 19:25-42; 20; 21
309	Nov 5	Acts 1; 2
310	Nov 6	Acts 3; 4
311	Nov 7	Acts 5; 6
312	Nov 8	Acts 7
313	Nov 9	Acts 8; 9
314	Nov 10	Acts 10
315	Nov 11	Acts 11
316	Nov 12	Acts 12; 13
317	Nov 13	Acts 14; 15; Galatians 1
318	Nov 14	Galatians 2; 3; 4
319	Nov 15	Galatians 5; 6; James 1
320	Nov 16	James 2; 3; 4; 5
321	Nov 17	Acts 16; 17
322	Nov 18	Acts 18:1-11; 1 Thessalonians 1; 2; 3; 4

323	Nov 19	1 Thessalonians 5;
		2 Thessalonians 1; 2; 3
324	Nov 20	Acts 18:12-28; 19:1-22;
		1 Corinthians 1
325	Nov 21	1 Corinthians 2; 3; 4; 5
326	Nov 22	1 Corinthians 6; 7; 8
327	Nov 23	1 Corinthians 9; 10; 11
328	Nov 24	1 Corinthians 12; 13; 14
329	Nov 25	1 Corinthians 15; 16
330	Nov 26	Acts 19:23-41; 20:1;
		2 Corinthians 1; 2
331	Nov 27	2 Corinthians 3; 4; 5
332	Nov 28	2 Corinthians 6; 7; 8; 9
333	Nov 29	2 Corinthians 10; 11; 12
334	Nov 30	2 Corinthians 13; Romans 1; 2
335	Dec 1	Romans 3; 4; 5
336	Dec 2	Romans 6; 7; 8
337	Dec 3	Romans 9; 10; 11

338	Dec 4	Romans 12; 13; 14
339	Dec 5	Romans 15; 16
340	Dec 6	Acts 20:2-38; 21
341	Dec 7	Acts 22; 23
342	Dec 8	Acts 24; 25; 26
343	Dec 9	Acts 27; 28
344	Dec 10	Ephesians 1; 2; 3
345	Dec 11	Ephesians 4; 5; 6
346	Dec 12	Colossians 1; 2; 3
347	Dec 13	Colossians 4; Philippians 1; 2
348	Dec 14	Philippians 3; 4; Philemon
349	Dec 15	1 Timothy 1; 2; 3; 4
350	Dec 16	1 Timothy 5; 6; Titus 1; 2
351	Dec 17	Titus 3; 2 Timothy 1; 2; 3
352	Dec 18	2 Timothy 4; 1 Peter 1; 2
353	Dec 19	1 Peter 3; 4; 5; Jude
354	Dec 20	2 Peter 1; 2; 3; Hebrews 1
355	Dec 21	Hebrews 2; 3; 4; 5

356	Dec 22	Hebrews 6; 7; 8; 9
357	Dec 23	Hebrews 10; 11
358	Dec 24	Hebrews 12; 13; 2 John; 3 John
359	Dec 25	1 John 1; 2; 3; 4
360	Dec 26	1 John 5; Revelation 1; 2
361	Dec 27	Revelation 3; 4; 5; 6
362	Dec 28	Revelation 7; 8; 9; 10; 11
363	Dec 29	Revelation 12; 13; 14; 15
364	Dec 30	Revelation 16; 17; 18; 19
365	Dec 31	Revelation 20; 21; 22

You have completed the entire Bible-Congratulations!

MAJORING IN MEN® CURRICULUM

MANHOOD GROWTH PLAN

Order the corresponding workbook for each book, and study the first four Majoring In Men® Curriculum books in this order:

MAXIMIZED MANHOOD: Realize your need for God in every area of your life and start mending relationships with Christ and your family.

COURAGE: Make peace with your past, learn the power of forgiveness and the value of character. Let yourself be challenged to speak up for Christ to other men.

COMMUNICATION, SEX AND MONEY: Increase your ability to communicate, place the right values on sex and money in relationships, and greatly improve relationships, whether married or single.

STRONG MEN IN TOUGH TIMES: Reframe trials, battles and discouragement in light of Scripture and gain solid footing for business, career, and relational choices in the future.

Choose five of the following books to study next. When you have completed nine books, if you are not in men's group, you can find a Majoring In Men® group near you and become "commissioned" to minister to other men.

DARING: Overcome fear to live a life of daring ambition for Godly pursuits.

SEXUAL INTEGRITY: Recognize the sacredness of the sexual union, overcome mistakes and blunders and commit to righteousness in your sexuality.

UNIQUE WOMAN: Discover what makes a woman tick, from adolescence through maturity, to be able to minister to a spouse's uniqueness at any age.

NEVER QUIT: Take the ten steps for entering or leaving any situation, job, relationship or crisis in life.

REAL MAN: Discover the deepest meaning of Christlikeness and learn to exercise good character in times of stress, success or failure.

POWER OF POTENTIAL: Start making solid business and career choices based on Biblical principles while building core character that affects your entire life.

ABSOLUTE ANSWERS: Adopt practical habits and pursue Biblical solutions to overcome "prodigal problems" and secret sins that hinder both success and satisfaction with life.

TREASURE: Practice Biblical solutions and principles on the job to find treasures such as the satisfaction of exercising integrity and a job well done.

IRRESISTIBLE HUSBAND: Avoid common mistakes that sabotage a relationship and learn simple solutions and good habits to build a marriage that will consistently increase in intensity for decades.

CHURCH GROWTH PLAN
STRONG - SUSTAINABLE - SYNERGISTIC
THREE PRACTICAL PHASES TO A POWERFUL MEN'S MOVEMENT IN YOUR CHURCH

Phase One:

- Pastor disciples key men/men's director using Maximized Manhood system.

- Launch creates momentum among men

- Church becomes more attractive to hold men who visit

- Families grow stronger

- Men increase bond to pastor

Phase Two:

- Men/men's director teach other men within the church

- Increased tithing and giving by men

- Decreased number of families in crisis

- Increased mentoring of teens and children

- Increase of male volunteers

- Faster assimilation for men visitors - clear path for pastor to connect with new men

- Men pray regularly for pastor

Phase Three:

- Men teach other men outside the church and bring them to Christ

- Increased male population and attraction to a visiting man, seeing a place he belongs

- Stronger, better-attended community outreaches

- Men are loyal to and support pastor

This system enables the pastor to successfully train key leaders,

create momentum, build a church that attracts and holds men

who visit, and disciple strong men.

Churches may conduct men's ministry entirely free of charge!

Learn how by calling 817-437-4888.

SPECIAL NOTE

Unique Woman book and curriculum has proven successful with women studying alone or with friends. It's been used by both men's and women's groups, as well as with couples.

If you study as a couple outside of a class situation, work separately, then compare notes to see what you've learned. Where you have differences, dig deeper into Scripture, utilizing the "For Further Study" section. Then pray together and come into a place of agreement. Sometimes a troublesome issue early in the book is resolved by the end of the book. If you struggle as a couple, seek your pastor's help.

CONTACT
MAJORING IN MEN® CURRICULUM
817-437-4888
admin@ChristianMensNetwork.com

Christian Men's Network
P.O. Box 93478
Southlake, TX 76092

Great discounts available.

Start your discipleship TODAY!

Call today for group discounts
and coaching opportunities.

FREE DVD!
Send your name and address to:
office@ChristianMensNetwork.com
We'll send you a FREE full-length DVD
with ministry for men.
(Limit one per person.)

ABOUT THE AUTHORS

Edwin Louis Cole, together with his wife Nancy Corbett Cole and their family, built a global organization called Christian Men's Network that "majored in men" in ministry.

Edwin Louis Cole mentored hundreds of thousands of people through challenging events and powerful books that have become the most widely-used Christian men's resources in the world. He is known for pithy statements and a confrontational style that demanded social responsibility and family leadership.

After serving as a pastor, evangelist, and Christian television pioneer, and at an age when most men were retiring, he followed his greatest passion—to lead men into Christlikeness, which he called "real manhood."

Ed Cole was a real man through and through. A loving son to earthly parents and the heavenly Father. Devoted husband to the "loveliest lady in the land," Nancy Corbett Cole. Dedicated father to three and, over the years, accepting the role of "father" to thousands. A reader, a thinker, a visionary. A man who made mistakes, learned lessons, then shared the wealth of his wisdom with men around the world. The Christian Men's Network he founded in 1977 is still a vibrant, global ministry. Unquestionably, he was the greatest men's minister of his generation.

Facebook.com/EdwinLouisCole